WENT MISSING
REDUX
Unsolved Great Lakes Shipwrecks

Frederick Stonehouse

Avery Color Studios, Inc.
Gwinn, Michigan

©2008 Avery Color Studios, Inc.

ISBN-13: 978-1-892384-45-4
ISBN-10: 1-892384-45-0

Library of Congress Control Number: 2007943880

First Edition 2008

10 9 8 7 6 5 4 3 2 1

Published by
Avery Color Studios, Inc.
Gwinn, Michigan 49841

Cover photos: Author's Collection

No portion of this publication may be reproduced, reprinted or otherwise copied for distribution purposes without written permission of the publisher.

Table Of Contents

Introduction 1

Captain's Napier's Last Trip - The *Alpena* (1880) 7

Lost off the Keweenaw - the *Manistee* (1883) 25

Questions, Always Questions - the *W.H. Gilcher* (1892) . . 37
    Addendum To Cracking *Gilcher* 49

Lost off the Keweenaw - the *Hudson* (1901) 53

A Victim of Superior Shoal? - The *Bannockburn* (1902) . . 67

"Freshwater, Bah!" - the *Adella Shores* (1909) 81

"Bucking Into the Teeth of the Gale," -
    the *Henry B. Smith* (1913) 91

C'est Le Guerre - the *Inkermann* and *Cerisoles*[i] (1918) . . 117
    Addendum To *Inkermann* and *Cerisoles* 133

Too Small to do the Job - the *Lambton* (1922) 153

End Notes 169

Bibliographic Notes 187

About The Author 199

"'It is the War'"

INTRODUCTION

The original *Went Missing* as published in 1977 only dealt with Lake Superior ship losses. Based on its success I later expanded the concept in 1984 into all of the Great Lakes with *Went Missing II*. It also enjoyed success. However research is a never-ending process and as more information came to light regarding the various shipwrecks I decided it was time to update the *Went Missing* premise yet again. The result is *Went Missing Redux*. For readers not familiar with the term "redux" it is Latin meaning "brought back," or "revisited," certainly very appropriate given the approach and historic nature of the shipwrecks.

Some of the stories are deeply analytical while others are briefer. All deal with ships that have never been found, or at least discovery has never been substantiated.

I predicated my missing ships on two considerations:

1. The vessels were lost with all hands in an unknown location and remain undiscovered. The ships may have "disappeared" before someone's eyes but given individual circumstances that doesn't mean witnessing an actual sinking. I didn't consider observer reports of a vessel "in trouble" to be accounts of a definite sinking. If the observer didn't see the ship sink into the water, it didn't happen.

2. The exact cause of loss is unknown. While we can usually assume a storm loss, what was the specific reason for the sinking? Did the cargo shift with a capsizing result? Could the hull have fractured due to stress or brittle steel? Or was it a combination of factors?

Ancillary to the criteria is the idea that if the loss didn't especially interest me, I didn't include it. An example of this is the long lost *Griffon* (aka *Grifon*, *Griffen*, *Griffin*, etc.). The small brig was built by the French explorer Rene-Robert Cavalier Sieur de La Salle at Niagara on Lake Erie in 1679. After sailing to the Green Bay area on Lake Michigan, La Salle loaded the *Griffon* with furs intended to finance his continued North American explorations and sent her back to Niagara. She never arrived, disappearing en route with all hands. Historians have often placed the wreck in northern Lake Michigan with some even ranging as far as northern Lake Huron. Over the years the *Griffon* has been "found" perhaps a dozen times but after investigation each proved to be the wreckage of another vessel. The latest reported "find" is thought by many experts to be nothing but a pond net stake protruding from the bottom. But discovery, like beauty, is in the eye of the beholder so the finder is convinced of the correctness of his cause. Since the *Griffon* was the first European ship to "go missing" on the Lakes, she will certainly be found, again and again! She has been called the "Holy Grail" of Great Lakes shipwrecks and like that mythical cup remains lost to man. Hordes of would-be Lancelots continue to seek it with as much success as the original knight (but at least he got good Queen Guinevere).

The Griffon *is considered the "holy grail" of Great Lakes shipwrecks. She was the first European vessel to "go missing" on the lakes.* Author

While any vessel lost with all hands has an inherent degree of mystery attached, this book isn't an attempt to "build mystery" into any of the losses. I do reserve the right to use a pinch of poetic license but only when plainly obvious. Sea monsters didn't sink the ships and swallow the crews nor space

Introduction

aliens abduct them to another world. None fell victim to "Great Lakes Triangles" or similar weirdness.

The reader must take extreme care in making any comparison between these vessels that "went missing" on the Great Lakes and those lost in the inane hoax of the "Bermuda Triangle." In the case of the Great Lakes there is no evidence of supernatural involvement. Of course there isn't any in the "Bermuda Triangle" either but that hasn't stopped legions of hack writers, unbalanced spiritualists and outright crooks and charlatans from capitalizing on public gullibility.

As I complained in my 1984 introduction a great problem of historical research as needed for this volume is completeness. Research can become an end unto itself. It can continue "ad nauseam," or it can halt at a reasonable point. The danger of not stopping at some reasonable point or establishing a clear cut off is obvious. However the reader should be aware serious research about the great Egyptian pyramids is ongoing hundreds of years and scholars still can't agree as to their purpose. Some of the folks even claim they were giant markers for a UFO spaceport but then this leads us back to the Bermuda Triangle nonsense.

For me the book has been an exercise in research, accumulating and evaluating data in an effort to gain greater insight into some of the most baffling shipwrecks on the Great Lakes. The complete investigation into these losses isn't yet finished and will not be until their dead hulks are found and they finally yield their long held secrets to the world. And they certainly will be found. The search technology of today would have been science fiction 50 years ago. Certainly what we will have in future, near and far term, will be beyond our dreams.

In some of the stories I was highly speculative, but I tried to keep the speculation tied closely to historical perspective. I never used it to spice a tale and clearly, it is obvious when I am venturing from the facts.

The idea for the original 1977 book came from the November 1913 wreck of the *Henry B. Smith*, one of the great mysteries of the lakes. While I was trying to pull together a coherent theory of loss and a good X marking the theoretical spot of the wreck, I conjectured if all available data from other "went missing" wrecks could be assembled and analyzed, could historians render valid conclusions regarding the losses? Could they solve the mystery?

In some ways this book is an effort to do just that. Whether I succeeded or failed is strictly up to you, the reader.

Writing a book like *Went Missing Redux* (or the earlier two) is a bit dangerous. After all I am often hypothesizing where the undiscovered wrecks will be found. Given the current level of search technology and the anticipated improvements, the lost ships will be found. If located where I suggested they are, I'm a genius (or a very lucky guesser). If not, I'm not, but as an old mob enforcer once said, "thems da breaks!".

To a point I have tried to challenge the reader, to make him think. If he concludes my thoughts regarding the evidence are wrong, let him reason otherwise and reach his own conclusions. There are many ways to skin a cat.

It is interesting to realize that not for the circumstances of foundering in relatively modern times (1975) when comparatively high technology search devices including state of the art magnetic anomaly detectors (MAD) on Navy P-3 Orion aircraft and towed side scan sonar were readily available, the *Edmund Fitzgerald* would have been part of the went missing fleet. Even at this writing, 33 years after the wreck, the reason for the loss of the "good ship and crew," remain controversial. Place the loss in 1900 and she likely would still be missing.

There were two earlier wrecks that just by the grace of God would have fallen into the went missing category too. The 623-foot freighter *Carl D. Bradley* was downbound on Lake Michigan in rolling gale on November 18, 1958 when she suddenly snapped in two. Only two men of the 35 aboard survived. Had the Coast Guard not plucked them from their open life raft as quickly as they did, there would have been no survivors to tell the tale of the demise of the steamer, a missing ship and two dead men on a life raft!

Eight years later the 580-foot freighter *Daniel J. Morrell* did the same trick, breaking in two in November gale on Lake Huron. Only a single man of her 29-man crew lived to tell the world what happened and again only the last minute arrival of a Coast Guard helicopter saved him from joining his messmates on the bottom of the lake.

It is safe to assume that if any of these three wrecks, the *Fitzgerald*, *Morrell* or *Bradley* happened fifty years before there would have been no survivors and all would be chapters in *Went Missing Redux*.

It is important to understand ships don't usually wreck for a single reason. Invariably the wreck is the result of a combination of events, a chain of circumstance that if broken by man or happenstance, halts or materially alters the disaster.

For example a captain makes a bad decision and starts his trip in spite of the forecast of a powerful storm. In his defense experience has demonstrated to him the weather forecasts are usually wrong or at least much less severe than claimed. Plus ships make money by carrying cargo between ports, not hiding in harbor every time it gets rough. In this instance the forecasts are spot on and the captain and ship are caught in the storm of their lives. Regardless of the ferocity of the storm the captain is skillful and ship well

Introduction

The 623-foot Carl D. Bradley, *lost on Lake Michigan in November 1958. Author*

built and maintained. Both should survive without significant problems. However, a rouge wave smashes into the ship and she heels more than normal causing her grain cargo to suddenly shift. Now listing badly, her rudder is largely out of the water and ineffective. The list makes it virtually impossible for firemen in the engine room to keep shoveling coal to the boiler fires and the ship slowly loses power to both engines and pumps. Listing heavily the ship is exposed to waves sweeping up the spar deck and crashing against the forward cabin. Over time doors are hammered in and water begins slowly making its way below decks. Since there is no steam available to power the pumps, the water continues to accumulate adding to the list. The more water in the ship, the deeper in the water she rides becoming more vulnerable to the waves. The water in the ship increases her heel and the covers of her many hatches are slowly being forced off by the breaking waves. As the hatch covers are swept away waves flood into the cargo holds. She is an utterly doomed ship. Since the list is so extreme the crew is unable to launch lifeboats. The lower side boat was long since been swept away by the seas and the high side one is unusable since it is virtually trapped in its davits by its very weight. Every man will be lost.

WENT MISSING REDUX

Had the captain not left port, storm not been so intense, the watchmen seen the rouge wave coming allowing the captain to quarter it, the wave not rolled her farther over than expected, grain not shifted or been better trimmed, rudder not lost control, engines and pumps not failed, forward doors remained secure, hatches been better secured and remained battened, the ship may have survived the storm. If the low lee side lifeboat had not been swept away, perhaps even with the ship lost, a crewman could have lived to tell the tale. If she had a radio the captain could have called for help but once the engines died so did the electric power unless of course it had an emergency battery backup and the antenna remained useable and pilothouse house not flooded out from waves smashing in the forward windows. The chain can be nearly endless.

As a point of explanation, I used the terms "ship," "vessel" and "boat" interchangeably. While most folks will agree ship and vessel are the same, boat jars them a bit. Old Navy guys will chant boats go on ships and certainly aren't the same. However there is a long tradition on the Great Lakes of calling anything that floats a boat, be it a 12-foot pram or 1,000-foot bulk freighter. I chose to honor the tradition.

I hope you enjoy reading *Went Missing Redux* and perhaps speculating on the stories of the ships that sailed off into a crack in the lake.

Captain Napier's Last Trip - The *Alpena*

Half-mast the starry flags to-day!
Bells, peal your sad funeral dirge!
A sailor bold has pass'd away,
Whelm'd Michigan, beneath thy surge.

A braver seaman never trod.
Supreme, upon the "peopled deck" -
True to his wife, his friends and God
He perished in the *Alpena's* wreck!

So began a poem by Captain Sam Ward dedicated to Captain Nelson W. Napier, the master of the Goodrich sidewheeler *Alpena*. During his career Captain Napier built a reputation as the best skipper in the Goodrich fleet. An outstanding seaman, his vessels were popular with passengers, crew and shippers alike.[i]

Napier came from a true sailing family. Uncles Joseph and John Napier were also lake skippers. As a boy he frequently sailed with both and learned the way of the lakes at a very early age. His own career with the Goodrich Transportation Company started as a wheelsman, advancing in order to third mate, second mate, chief mate and finally captain. He spent much of his time running across Lake Michigan, usually from Muskegon and Grand Haven, Michigan to Chicago. As a result he knew his sailing area very, very well. You could say he was even groomed for it! In 45 years as a captain he supposedly never lost a ship, excellent record in an age when shipwreck was commonplace and a captain losing a ship not necessarily a disgrace. When he

WENT MISSING REDUX

The burning of the Sea Bird *on April 9, 1868 was a shock to the traveling public. Author*

went down with the *Alpena* he was 67 years old and left a wife and two young children at home in St. Joseph, Michigan. He also had three grown sons and a daughter from an earlier marriage.

The Goodrich Company was considered one of the best, if not the best transportation firm on the Great Lakes. The fleet vessels were thought reliable, safe and very well run. In view of this stellar reputation among the traveling public, the burning of the *Seabird* off Waukegan, Illinois in April 1868 with the loss of 102 passengers and crew was shocking but not unheard of.

In August 1860 perhaps 300 people were lost when the *Lady Elgin* foundered in Lake Michigan. Three years prior the steamer *Montreal* burned in the St. Lawrence River just a few miles from Lake Ontario with a death toll of 250 folks. The *Northern Indiana* went up in flames in 1856 on Lake Erie resulting in the death of 35-56 of the 175 aboard. When the propeller *Atlantic* sank after a collision on Lake Erie 250 passengers and crew perished. And of course the mother of all American shipping losses, the burning of the paddlewheeler *Sultana* on the Mississippi with over 1,500 Union soldiers killed in 1865 was well known.[ii] So when it was placed in perspective, the *Seabird* tragedy, while horrible, was not terribly unusual.

Captain Albert E. Goodrich purchased the sidewheeler *Alpena* from Gardner, Ward and Gallagher for $80,000 to replace the lost *Seabird* . Built by Thomas Arnold in Marine City, Michigan in 1867 the *Alpena* was 197-feet

Captain Napier's Last Trip - The Alpena

Was the Alpena *rammed and sunk by the schooner* D.A. Wells *in a repeat of the* Augusta-Lady Elgin *disaster? Author*

The loss of Sultana *by explosion and fire on the Mississippi River in 1865 with over 1,500 Union soldiers, many wounded, was the greatest shipwreck loss in U.S. history. Author*

long with a depth of 12-feet. Although the vessel was not built specifically for Goodrich as he usually demanded, she was acceptable under the circumstances for his intended use. Her machinery came from the Detroit Locomotive Works and consisted of a single cylinder vertical beam engine with a 44-inch by eleven-foot stroke driving sidewheels with a radius of 24-feet. Under good conditions the engine and wheels could propel her at about 15 knots. Normal crew size was about 25 men.

The *Alpena* was a very typical Great Lakes sidewheeler, her profile dominated by her huge "walking beam" steam engine with the stack forward of the wheels. A long wooden arch providing longitudinal strength, dominated the center of the vessel. Passengers generally kept to the upper deck while freight was confined to the main deck below. Gangways were big enough to permit freight wagons to back right up to them allowing an efficient transfer of cargo, making for quick turnarounds in port. A very small pilothouse was perched forward. She was named for Alpena, Michigan, a small Lake Huron mill town.

Goodrich used the *Alpena* on a variety of routes including servicing the ports along the east shore of Lake Michigan. Most commonly though she steamed between Grand Haven, Muskegon and Chicago. The regular schedule required her to first load at the Central Wharf in Muskegon in the late afternoon and run to Grand Haven a dozen miles to the south. After loading she usually pulled away from the city around 10:00 p.m. and headed across the lake for Chicago. The trip was about 105 miles on roughly a south-southwest heading and by early morning she was typically safely moored to

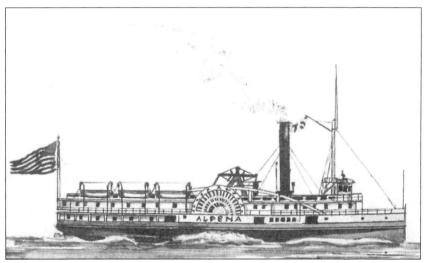

The sidewheeler Alpena. *Author*

Captain Napier's Last Trip - The Alpena

The Alpena *usually met her fleet mate* Muskegon *in mid Lake Michigan on her crossing. Author*

her Chicago dock. If the lake was calm, it was a pleasant and comfortable excursion for passengers and crew. If gales and storms ruled the water, it was tough steamboating for all.

She often ran in tandem with another Goodrich steamer, *Muskegon,* and during night crossings the two vessels met mid-lake and ran close enough to signal with loud whistle blasts.

Napier and the *Alpena* began their last trip on October 15, 1880. As normal they ran from Muskegon to Grand Haven, loaded the last of the passengers and freight, departing the latter port about 9:30 p.m.

The weather on the open lake was nearly perfect, a small easy swell from a light northerly breeze being the only blemish. The day was a perfect example of "Indian Summer" weather. Temperatures ranged from 65-70 degrees, a far cry from the normal October chill.

The *Alpena* swiftly churned along into the calm night, driving ever onward to Chicago. At 1:00 a.m. she exchanged the customary whistle signals with the *Muskegon*, much to the annoyance of sleeping passengers. Everything was normal, just as it should be except it was the last time the fleet mates ever exchanged greetings.

Shortly after the two ships passed, weather conditions changed abruptly as a powerful low pressure system swept out of the southwest. From the reported weather conditions it was soon apparent what the *Alpena* faced. Within an hour the temperatures plummeted from a pleasant 65 degrees to a frigid 32. A demon wind blowing straight from the bowels of hell screamed over the lake. Manitowoc measured the wind at 70 miles per hour, creating terrifying waves and blinding snow squalls. Tremendous seas crashed into the *Muskegon's* quarter rolling down her decks and carrying away all manner of loose and poorly secured gear. Wind driven spume and spray froze to her superstructure, rigging, spars, lifeboats and pilothouse windows. It can only be assumed Captain Napier on the *Alpena* continued to punch through the storm toward Chicago. Remember the *Muskegon* was running with the seas on her stern, usually a much easier point of steaming than battling them head on as the *Alpena's* course required.

Ports everywhere on Lake Michigan were being ravaged by the storm. In Milwaukee buildings were blown down and the harbor turned into a maelstrom. Further west a blizzard dumped drifts of snow a dozen feet high, paralyzing railroads.

The winds began in Chicago with force around 3:00 a.m. and by 6:00 a.m. reached hurricane strength. Factory walls tumbled to the ground and an empty box car was blown from its tracks slamming into a passing train! Ships thought safely moored in the river had hawsers snap like too taught rubber bands and driven into other vessels creating a massive floating snarl.

Grand Haven too was smashed by the storm. One woman later wrote, "When the boat left Friday evening it was as fine a night as one would wish to see: bright moonlight, a quiet sea, everything promising a fortunate trip across the lake. At two o'clock that night I was awakened by a sound, which shook the whole house, a mighty blow, inflicted by a giant's hand. The wind ravaged and shrieked outside and came with such force against our west windows that my husband rose early and nailed some heavy old doors from the barn over our west windows but even then it was impossible to keep out the blast. A driving snowstorm set in so one could scarcely see past his nose. I never shall forget that Saturday morning when I huddled near the old kitchen stove, my baby in my arms, the tears running down my face, dreading I knew not what, but instinctively feeling from the fiendish violence of the storm and its untimeliness, it being only the middle of October, that something terrible was fairly soon to occur."

Holland was slammed too. A cornice blew off the City Hotel nearly destroying the structure. Homes lost roofs and 25-foot waves knocked the breakwater light off its foundations.

The south pier lighthouse was also destroyed by wind and wave and nearly all of the piles of milled lumber were blown down in Muskegon.

Captain Napier's Last Trip - The Alpena

Cana Island Light in Wisconsin just to the south of the "Door" was hit hard with water flooding through a window ten feet above the foundation, forcing the keeper and his family to flee to the boathouse for safety.[iii]

The storm was equally devasting at other points too! Numerous trains were stalled by wind driven snow packing drifts so tight as to block the rails. Roads were drifted shut and rescue parties in sleighs fought their way through the snow to stalled trains with emergency supplies.

The *Alpena* wasn't alone on the lake that fateful night. The sudden storm front inflicted tremendous damage on the lakes fleet. Some 94 vessels representing every class from barges to schooners to powerful propellers were damaged or wrecked and approximately 118 people reported killed. Since records of who was actually aboard a given ship were often incomplete, the true number lost will never be known with absolute certainty. Between Kewaunee, Wisconsin and Death's Door on the Door Peninsula, an expanse of only 50 miles, 20 vessels wrecked!

The propeller *Canisteo* sank off Waugoshance Shoals north of the Manitou Passage after colliding with the schooner *George Murray* in zero visibility, the schooner *Nahob* ashore at Cana Island, schooners *Reciprocity* and *Hungaria* on the rocks off Two Rivers and bark *Captain William Thompson* lost in the breakers, schooner-barge *Florence Lester* wrecked with six men off Manistee, schooner *Australia* smashed on a nearby sandbar; the list of wrecked and damaged vessels and dead crew and passengers seemed endless.

When the *Alpena* failed to arrive in Chicago in the morning as scheduled no immediate fear was felt. After all, the storm had been fierce and surely she was just delayed or perhaps even put into another port to wait out the weather. However storm reports from possible harbors of refuge made such action all but impossible.

The *Oconto*, another Goodrich vessel, was also caught in the clench of the great storm. Battered and ice covered with damaged topsides and missing lifeboats swept off by wind and wave, her late arrival at Manitowoc caused considerable worry. But at least it was "better late than never." The *Oconto* earlier gained a measure of fame when she blew a head gasket in 1878. Her engineer calmly cut a new one out of a wood gangway plank and fitted it tightly enough to allow her to continue to the next port.[iv]

The propeller *De Pere*, another Goodrich boat, was 25 miles off Grand Haven, bound in from Milwaukee, when the storm smashed into her about 3:00 a.m. Captain Pittman knew he couldn't keep control of the ship if he tried to enter the narrow channel into port so he turned north battling the seas for 12 hours until he was able to make Manistee and safety. He later estimated his chances of making it through the Manistee piers at only 50-50 but he had no choice but to try. Luckily he had the right 50. Passengers were so impressed with the skill and courage of the ship's officers they took up a cash collection and presented it to them after safely mooring to the solid dock.

Although publicly confident, the people at the Goodrich office were certainly feeling sharp twinges of concern over the missing *Alpena*. When the *Muskegon* returned from Grand Haven to Chicago she kept a sharp watch for any evidence of the absent *Alpena*, as did the *Menominee* running from Milwaukee to Grand Haven. They saw nothing of her. A chartered vessel was also dispatched by the company to search the Manitou, Beaver and Fox Islands area. Wreckage was reported everywhere, but none could be specifically identified with the missing *Alpena*. With 94 vessels wrecked or damaged, flotsam littered the lake.

By October 19th it was obvious the ship was lost in the storm. Wreckage marked *Alpena* was finally found near Holland on the east shore of Lake Michigan. Included were fire buckets, a grand piano minus the lid, cabin doors, stenciled life jackets and a large quantity of apples. She carried four carloads of apples as well as eight carloads of mattress stuffing and an unknown quantity of Grand Rapids made furniture including wooden coffins.[v] The coffins were especially valuable to the beach scavengers but more on them later.

Goodrich officials positively acknowledged the Holland area wreckage from the *Alpena* and accepted it as proof positive she was lost. Until then the barest flame of hope still flickered. Some of the wreckage today is is at the Holland Museum.

Local beachcombers had a field day with all the flotsam. Marked life jackets were reportedly selling for $5 each.[vi] What a great souvenir of the wreck! Some folks later claimed many of the life jackets aboard were rotten and valueless in an emergency. The truth of this claim is unknown. One scavenger tore a gold painted sign with flowery decoration from part of a cabin section but authorities managed to "capture" it before a scavenger stole it. Another forager grabbed the gilded gold and brass ball from the top of a paddle box and refused to sell it for any price. What he thought he would do with it was anyone's guess. The wholesale looting of the wreckage by local folks made the investigator's job all the more difficult. Evidence that perhaps could help explain what happened was being stolen left and right!

The following day the body of a woman washed ashore about five miles north of Holland. Although apparently never identified, she was thought to be from the *Alpena*. On the 21st the body of a boy about eight years old was discovered in the same general area. It is also unclear whether he was ever identified.

Captain Napier's Last Trip - The **Alpena**

With the news wreckage from the *Alpena* was coming ashore, Holland was soon crowded with bereaved relatives of passengers and crew, many coming via special train from Grand Haven. City livery stables did a brisk business hiring out rigs to carry the searchers to the storm tossed beaches to look for the remains of their loved ones. Some of the grief stricken people walked the lakeshore for weeks, hoping for the impossible, to find their loved one "-coming ashore." Hotels and boarding houses like the Phoenix and Ottawa House filled with searchers, all waiting for the next discovery. In a way their loss was Holland's business gain but this is true in all such tragedies.

Not all business profited. In spite of the huge number of people in town, a once popular light-hearted comedy went barely attended at the local theater. Apparently most people were too overwhelmed by the disaster to enjoy the show.

Captain Napier's three adult sons, all lake captains, arrived to search for his body as well as the hull of the ship. Originally it was thought the entire hull was ashore near the Holland harbor entrance but it later proved to be just a small section of it.

The Napier family offered a reward of $100 for the recovery of the captain's remains. Like most of those lost, it was reportedly never found.

Stealing the flotsam coming ashore became a local enterprise. Holland residents may present an attitude of holier than thou to the world based on their strong Dutch Reform bent, but it didn't prevent the age old practice of "scavenging" after a wreck. The locals of course claimed it was "outsiders" doing the dirty work! Surely it couldn't be them! The wooden caskets that came ashore were especially useful for scavengers since they were really nothing more than great big empty boxes. Fill'em up with all matter of "stuff," give a strong heave ho and a couple of stout fellows could easily carry away a bundle of goods.

Captain Thomas G. Butlin, the Superintendent of the Goodrich Company, was given the thankless task of organizing special patrols to search the beaches for bodies. In addition it was his responsibility to safeguard the valuables and other personal possessions washing onto the beach. It was an impossible task given the long stretch of shore and the constant scavenging of the locals. While Captain Butlin went about his gruesome search, the U.S. tug *Graham* located three floaters in a wreckage field in the still rough offshore waters.[vii]

Ten miles north of Holland the body of a Grand Rapids man was found on the sandy beach. In his pocket was a small scrap of paper bearing the hastily scrawled message, "we are having a terrible time of it, the steamer is breaking up." The note only stated the obvious.

WENT MISSING REDUX

Fixing the time of loss is relatively easy. Three of the bodies recovered had watches that stopped at about 10:50. It is presumed this means Saturday night. Watches during this period of technology were not waterproof in the slightest. If they touched water, they stopped! Finding three stopped at the same time was near certain proof of the time of loss.

Since no manifest was made, it can only be assumed that the *Alpena* was carrying about 100 passengers and crew. Some sources claim 60-100. It's all a guess but for this number of people, very few bodies were ever recovered, perhaps as few as six! The prevailing theory at the time was most were drifting along the lake bottom outside of near shore sand bars and prevented from washing ashore by strong lateral currents.

There was one quasi survivor to the *Alpena* but only because he failed to get on board before she sailed and had to switch to another ship. That said he did experience much of the storm the *Alpena* foundered in. In his words, "I started for Chicago on the *Groh* (apparently the *Michael Groh*) from South Haven... At 11 o'clock the storm struck us and from that moment or experience can hardly be imagined much less described... a squall swung us around into the hollow of the sea and we almost rolled over. It cracked all the beams in the upper works and water came into her cabins by the barrel full... Saturday morning the wind was blowing a hurricane and water was coming in very fast when we broke our bilge pump: the water got within two inches of her fires when we managed to get it going again. On Saturday night we had used up all our fuel and had to swing lumber (author's note - they were using part of her lumber cargo for fuel) to keep her fires and had to keep at it until we landed at Manitou Harbor on Sunday night... hundreds of miles from our original course... during this ordeal I had not a mouthful to eat or drink nor did I sleep... the captain and crew were all much discouraged and we all expected to go to the bottom of the lake without fail. I never was so happy to see anything as I was to see land." The *Michael Groh* lasted until November 22, 1895 when she was smashed against the Pictured Rocks in Lake Superior.[viii]

Many of the passengers on the *Alpena* were prominent people and their death was a shock to their communities.

Mrs. S. D. Cole of Ottawa, Illinois was the sister of the Frank Holbrook, the agent for Goodrich in Muskegon. Her body was recovered at Holland. As proof of the quick breakup of the ship, while she wore a life jacket, her shoes weren't laced, dress not fastened and her purse hastily stashed inside of her dress. A woman of her prominence would not normally be "caught dead" so attired. Clearly she must have been under extreme duress.

Christopher Kusterer was the son of the biggest beer brewer in Grand Rapids. The family advertised a large reward for anyone recovering his remains. Among a physical description it mentioned he wore a, "gold watch with gold chain and charm representing a barrel composed of gray agates with gold trimming." No one ever claimed the reward.[ix]

Montgomery Crossman was the foreman of the Stearns Manufacturing Company in Grand Haven. The company specialized in making windmills for farm applications. He was traveling to Chicago to be honored at the Chicago Exposition for his innovative designs.

Edgar Locke's body also came ashore. He was the local representative for Hills Brothers Coffee. Headquartered in Chicago, he was only on the boat because a delayed appointment in Grand Rapids prevented him from catching the train back home as he wanted.

Although not prominent in business or society, the loss of Mrs. John Osborn and her three children was equally overwhelming. Only the body of nine-year old John Jr. ever came ashore. The family had lived in Muskegon but husband John took a new engineering job in Chicago and they were on the way to meet him and start a new life. Doubtless John was at the Goodrich dock in Chicago waiting for the ship that never arrived.

Captain Hever V. Squier, Jr. from Grand Haven was a prominent local tug boat master. He was heading to Chicago to meet his wife and three young daughters who were visiting friends.

Mr. and Mrs. W. J. Benham were important residents of Grand Haven where the husband was the editor of the *Grand Haven Herald*. Two children were orphaned by their deaths.

While learning their loved ones perished in the wreck was devastating for everyone, some took the news especially hard. Mrs. Harry St. Clair, her husband lost on the wreck, was later committed to a Chicago insane asylum.

Reverend and Mrs. Farrel Hart were married only two days before the sinking of the *Alpena*. A Presbyterian minister, he and his bride were heading for Chicago where he was to take over the Sunday school branch of a major religious publishing house. Just as in the strange case of Mrs. Doctor Dupe and the *Wabuno*, the new Mrs. Hart begged her husband not to take the *Alpena* to Chicago. She had already lost two brothers to the lake and was deathly afraid of it. Reverend Hart would not be dissuaded, especially not by his wife, a mere woman! Hart was extremely stubborn and according to local tradition her parents had desperately opposed the marriage because of his refusal to ever consider any other point of view on anything other than his own. They clearly saw such domination of their daughter as nothing more than mental cruelty. But she would not hear reason. Love is blind and the marriage, much to the anguish of her parents, went through. It was too bad she couldn't have invented an illness and let her headstrong, "always right, reverend" meet his maker early, and alone!ˣ

A problem common to many early shipwrecks involving loss of life is well illustrated by the *Alpena* disaster; to give proper names the bodies recovered. For example, the remains of one woman were only identified by a sharp-eyed clerk who remembered selling her a trunk on the day the ship sailed. His recollection saved her from an unknown's grave.

In the hope unclaimed bodies could be identified local newspapers carried advertisements for weeks following the sinking. Officials also advertised when they had unknown floaters on their hands. One advertisement read in part, "about 22 years of age, about 5 feet, 8 inches high, short reddish brown hair, dressed in a laborer's suit, with No. 10 stoga shoes, one front tooth out, smooth face, figure of a ballet girl dancing on a globe tattooed in blue on right forearm." Such advertisements were common, not only for the *Alpena* but for many Great Lakes shipwrecks. Families also missing loved ones advertised too.

The big city papers either hired or sent reporters to Holland to provide the latest news of the disaster. The *Chicago Tribune*, *Chicago Daily News*, *Inter-Ocean* and *Detroit Daily News* made every effort to keep their readers informed, well or otherwise. Unfortunately this was also the beginning of the age of "Yellow Journalism" and these papers did their best to uphold the high traditions of their business. Translate that to mean they did their best to sell papers, just like today. "Truth" became of a variable commodity. Readers hungered for sensationalism and reporters and their papers did their best to provide it. The local Holland papers took great exception to the reporting of the big city papers, especially when they started to call the locals, "beachcombers" and charged them with benefiting from the disaster.

One out of town paper described Holland as a "town... which possesses all the dullness... and lacks much of the picturesqueness of old country Dutch settlement." Certainly an accurate statement but guaranteed to raise local hackles. Can you imagine anything worse than a reporter used to the action and excitement of Chicago being "stuck" in Holland, Michigan (then or now)?

Reflecting just a touch of righteous indignation, one local paper reported that the "correspondents feel highly elated with their important (?) mission: go snorting and strutting about as if they were bigger than Grant. Some of them, only beardless youths: they invented all the fiction they could conjure up in their young, giddy minds and thus slandered an honest people who have endeavored to do their duty."ˣⁱ Right.

Gradually information trickled in which helped trace the last movements of the ill-fated *Alpena*. Captain Ben Wheeler of the schooner *S. A. Irish*

Captain Napier's Last Trip - The Alpena

reported sighting her about 6 a.m. on October 16th, working through the screaming gale. The *Irish* was in dire straits herself having lost all her deckload of shingles. An hour or so later Captain George Boomsluiter of the big schooner-barge *City of Grand Haven* saw her about 35 miles east of Kenosha, Wisconsin. She appeared to be laboring heavily as she punched her way windward through the cresting seas. With her black hull, white upper works and bright red stack banded by black at the top, all Goodrich colors, there wasn't any doubt as to her identity.[xii]

Between 10 - 11 a.m. another schooner, believed to be the *Challenger* (although it could have been the *Holmes*), sighted her struggling in the trough of the waves. The *Alpena* was headed due west and although she flew no distress flag, it was evident she was in trouble. To the crew of the schooner it looked like the *Alpena* wasn't using her engine. The schooner, running under bare poles herself, was fighting to stay afloat and could offer no help to the *Alpena*.

Although no time or location was given a later report indicated an unidentified schooner sighted the *Alpena* laying on her side with one paddle out of the water, suggesting her cargo shifted.

It was thought the *Alpena* drifted the rest of the day, her lifeless hulk propelled by the merciless wind and waves. She traveled perhaps 15 or 20 miles before sinking, until a northwest wind shift blew her or her wreckage field close to the Michigan coast at Holland.

After closely examining the wreckage marine men in Holland were very certain the steamer broke up completely rather than sinking intact, pointing out the wreckage was scattered over a 20 mile stretch of beach and part of her stern was near the Holland Harbor.

Many of the vessels on Lake Michigan that day were not surprised by the mid October storm. Although the *Alpena* left port during calm conditions, warnings of the blow to come were given to her before sailing. But the intensity of the winds and snow squalls caught mariners off guard and they just weren't prepared for the hell-bender they got.

The normal post shipwreck rumors circulated following the loss and there were those who claimed her unfit for the conditions wrought by the storm. Generally the *Alpena* was considered a staunch and well-found vessel as evidenced by her 13 years of reliable service. She performed well and was soundly maintained and yet was not old enough to be considered worn out. She was dry-docked and rebuilt in Manitowoc during the winter of 1876-77 at a cost of $20,000 and was reported better than new when returned for the 1877 season.

WENT MISSING REDUX

The *Chicago Tribune* reporter in Holland claimed most of the small broken pieces of wood coming ashore were rotten. Whether this claim was true or just typical "sensational" reporting isn't known. But when Captain Napier's son Ed looked at some of the arch timber wreckage he reportedly found them made with pine. If pine was used in the arches could it have been used in the hull? In his view only oak was acceptable. Was pine used in the 1876-77 rebuilt! Both Captain Goodrich and the shipyard later said no but that didn't squelch the rumors of a rotten boat. The U.S. Steamboat Inspectors who checked her in 1880 denied the pine claim too, saying their tests showed only oak as it should be.

The *Alpena* was once dry-docked at Milwaukee for repair to her steering chain and there were those folks who thought her chain may have failed again, causing her to fall off into the deadly wave trough. While a possibility there is no hard evidence to support the theory. In view of other, more likely causes, it must be relegated to a lower order of probability.

The more likely cause of loss is in the basic design of the vessel. Many marine men felt a sidewheeler was unsafe in truly heavy seas, the huge sidewheels lacking the power to battle though the waves. With the vessel rolling wildly in the seaway, one paddlewheel would bite deeply into the water while the other was lifted clear. The alternating of the wheels into and out of the water placed tremendous strain on the machinery connecting rods and shafts. By contrast a propeller turning under the surface with a rudder directly aft, provided far more effective power and maneuverability with much less strain. Reportedly Captain Napier had reservations about sidewheels in heavy sea conditions too but whether such rumors are fact or just dockside hindsight is undetermined.

During the early years of steam on the Great Lakes sidewheelers were common and popular with the public and shipping companies. Cargo space was plentiful and easily accessible and the beamy sidewheelers were usually very comfortable vessels for passengers. The opposing sidewheels provided good mobility in harbors and rivers too. By the turn of the century the sidewheelers largely died out, replaced by more efficient propellers.

The fortuitous discovery of notes in bottles after shipwrecks must always be viewed with some suspicion. Many have proved to be hoaxes but other times they were likely authentic. The July following the *Alpena* loss the keeper at Point Betsie Life-Saving Station 120 miles north of Grand Haven, reportedly found a bottle with a message sealed within. It was never determined if the message was genuine or a fake. If however it is real, it helps explain the conditions of loss. "October 16, 3 o'clock, on board the *Alpena* -

Captain Napier's Last Trip - The Alpena

she has broken her port wheel: is at mercy of the seas; is half full of water; God help us, Captain Napier washed overboard."

The note was signed by George A. N. Moore of Chicago and asked it to be delivered to his wife.

Two more victims also supposedly left messages. D. Caddie and Addie Kilson scribbled last messages on each side of a flimsy grape box top. The box top was discovered floating near the St. Joseph, Michigan piers. Caddie is thought to have scrawled, "Whoever picks this up remember the writer is only an orphan. I am happy and perfectly willing to die for I have no one to care for me now, or cherish my memory when I'm gone. At this time we all know our doom. The *S.S. Alpena* is very fast going to pieces. We know we will never reach land or ever see it again. Boat is going to pieces. 11:20." Whether such a long-winded moralistic last message is authentic or the creation of a short-on-copy "journalist" is anyone's guess. My bet goes on the "journalist." Kilson by contrast was succinct, "A few minutes more and we will be in a watery grave."

Captain Napier also reputedly sent a message. It was found scrawled on a piece of shingle about 11 inches by 4 inches and said, "The *Alpena* is going to pieces. We will all be lost." It was found by a little boy walking the beach five miles north of St. Joseph. It was heavily "sea washed" and some folks said there was also a reference to "gold" too but it was too faint to be read. Did she carry a secret cargo of gold? Treasure hunters would love that! All kidding aside, the Goodrich Company searched long and hard for the *Alpena's* safe. Many of the passengers deposited their valuables in it for security and the company had an obligation to return them to the various heirs and family members. The safe was apparently never located.

Messages in bottles could also be a prelude to fraud. For example, it seems two men identified the body of a Swede reportedly lost on the *Alpena* that came ashore near South Haven. Earlier newspaper stories reported he was insured for $4,000, a very considerable sum in 1880. So far so good but then two life insurance policies for the Swede naming the two "finders" as the beneficiaries show up in a bottle "discovered" on the beach near Muskegon. What an extraordinary stroke of luck! There is no record of either insurance pay out or arrest.[xiii]

After examining all the evidence and adding a healthy dose of his experience, Captain Goodrich determined the *Alpena* most likely foundered about 25 miles or so east of Kenosha. This location would be consistent with the wreckage field on the east shore as well as corresponding to the last reported position by other vessels. Unable to determine the exact cause of loss he concluded his steamer was simply overwhelmed by the fury of the storm.

He later provided a more detailed analysis. "We can theorize as much as we like and be very far from the facts. My idea is this - Captain Napier has been on the lake a great many years. He was known as a man of great courage. He would never allow himself to be beaten - to turn back in a gale. I think on the night of the storm his courage ran away with his judgment. He kept on his course too long and when he did turn back, absolutely compelled by the fury of the storm, the steamer dropped into the trough of the sea. Her cargo shifted to leeward. One of her wheels got out of the water. Captain Napier couldn't right her and she hammered along until she went down. In such circumstances nothing could have withstood such a storm. She had about ten carloads of freight on board and was naturally high out of the water, and exposed to the force of the wind.[xiv] In today's terms, Goodrich threw his captain under the bus! It was his fault, not the company's.

With the added variable of the storm causing machinery damage to one of the paddle wheels in turn causing her to fall into the wave trough, this writer would agree with Captain Goodrich concerning the technical reason at least.

A coroner's jury in Muskegon was far less charitable, holding the ship wasn't seaworthy and at least some of her life jackets were rotten. They also questioned the competence of the crew. Captain Napier and his chief engineer were long on experience but the rest of crew far less so. The jury found the Goodrich Transportation Company fully liable for the disaster.[xv]

There is also speculation the *Alpena* could have collided with the schooner *D.A. Wells*. The theory goes the steamer may have made it as far as Wind Point, north of Racine and turned northward to Kenosha with the intention of sheltering there.[xvi] However the big schooner *D.A. Wells* downbound with iron ore from Escanaba shot out of a wall of snow and slammed into her starboard side amidships, damaging the paddlewheel. Thus wounded, the *Alpena* fell off into the trough to eventually founder. The evidence is scant but there is some. The schooner was also heavily damaged, losing her bowsprit, foremast, part of her cabin and stove part of her hull. Later in the day a government ship noticed the schooner's obvious damage. The *Wells* later foundered with all hands seven miles northeast of Chicago. The tug *Little Giant*, seeing her signal from shore for help, went out to pick her up, but the schooner's lights disappeared before she arrived leaving no member of the crew alive to explain the damaged rigging seen by the tug.[xvii]

The argument she collided with the *Alpena* is essentially based on two factors. First, part of her cabin came ashore between Grand Haven and St. Joseph, the south end of the *Alpena* wreckage field. Therefore it can be suggested it was lost roughly the same time and in the same area the sidewheeler sank.

Captain Napier's Last Trip - The **Alpena**

Second, from the damage to the *Wells* she must have collided with something and another ship is the obvious choice. Losing a bowsprit is invariably the result of collision. If not the *Alpena* then who? The answer of course is any of the other ships lost in the storm, maybe.

The parallel with the *Augusta - Lady Elgin* disaster twenty years before is powerful. On September 7, 1860 the schooner *Augusta* rammed the sidewheeler *Lady Elgin* in a squall off Winnetka, Illinois, just north of Chicago. Initially thought not much injured, the steamer sank with the loss of an estimated 300 lives. When the schooner later struggled into Chicago her damages were similar to those reported suffered by the *Wells*. Was history repeating itself![xviii]

When all the conjecture and theories were complete the simple fact remains that Captain Nelson Napier and his passengers and crew were lost forever. Not a single survivor remained to tell the tale of her final desperate hours, or her final fate.

To commemorate the disastrous storm of October 1880 it is still referred to as the "*Alpena* Storm."

LOST OFF THE KEWEENAW - THE *MANISTEE*

The propeller *Manistee* was built in 1867 by E.M. Peck in Cleveland under contract for the Engelman Line of Milwaukee. The combination passenger and freight packet was 184-feet long and 677 tons, making her a respectably sized vessel for the times. She was initially used on Lake Michigan, running between Milwaukee on the Wisconsin shore and Michigan's Manistee, her route running approximately 100 miles across the lake. The run proved unprofitable and her owners decided the key to success was increasing her size so in 1871 she was cut amidships and a 30-foot long plug added to her center. Increasing the size of ships in this manner wasn't uncommon then or now. The "new" *Manistee* was given a fresh route between Grand Haven, Michigan and Milwaukee. The run required year around operation, which meant battering through winter ice when necessary, and the steamer proved generally equal to the task. On one occasion she couldn't work free from an ice jam and was caught in the ice for 58 days!

The term "propeller" referred to a type or vessel driven by a screw (screw propeller). The expression came into popular use in the 1860s as ships changed from sail and sidewheel to screw propulsion.

In 1872 she was acquired by Duluth interests, brought to the big lake and assigned the south shore run. The Ward Line later picked her up, shifting the route to between Duluth and Buffalo on Lake Erie. Leopold and Austrian purchased her in 1876 giving her a new run including Duluth, Houghton, Prince Arthur's Landing (today's Thunder Bay) and various intermediate stops.

To their credit the Steamboat Service Inspectors became concerned with the condition of the steamer and to address their anxiety she was drydocked

WENT MISSING REDUX

The Manistee *caught in an ice jam on Lake Michigan. Author*

at Manitowoc in the fall of 1879 at the Rand and Berger's Yard. Her captain, John McKay supervised the overhaul. Mastering her since her Ward Line days, he knew her strengths and weaknesses. Forty years old, he had a wife and two children at home in Cleveland.

The *Manistee's* upper works were completely rebuilt and new stanchions, plank sheers and topsides replaced including a substantial set of arches. The arches were needed to provide critical longitudinal strength to the wood hull and were a common feature for period steamers. Plank sheers, also called covering boards, are planks placed over the frames and sheer strake. Her hull was also repaired and replanked making her virtually a new ship. McKay was said to have implicit confidence in her.[i,ii]

Regardless of McKay's confidence, the boat still had problems. When placed back in service in 1881 she leaked badly through her concave sides when heavily loaded with freight. Since her sides were not removed during refit problems integral to them were uncorrected. The leaking was serious enough the ship was pulled out of service and sent to Chicago to the Miller Brothers Shipyard to have her sides taken down and a new frame installed and replanked. That this action was taken at the height of her summer trading season shows the importance of the work and that it couldn't be delayed until winter layup. Following the work insurance inspectors awarded her a rating of A-2, the highest possible for a steamer of her age.

Lost Off The Keweenaw - The Manistee

The *Manistee's* problems continued. In the fall of 1882 a major leak was discovered in her boiler water bottom. It was repaired to the tune of $4,000 while the steamer wintered in Duluth. When spring came the inspectors took a good look at her, liked what they saw and awarded her the same rating as previously.

Her career proceeded without incident until Saturday November 10, 1883 when she steamed out of Duluth with a cargo of flour, mill material and general freight consigned to Ontonagon and Portage, Michigan. Newspapers later claimed she carried 10,000 bushels of oats, 90 tons of mill feed, 1,254 barrels of flour, nine tons of general freight and an unknown amount of sashes and doors.[iii]

Sunday morning she arrived at Bayfield, Wisconsin at the base of the Apostle Islands about 75 lake miles east of Duluth. The weather was howling hard northwest and Captain McKay lost five long days waiting for the gale to blow itself out. Every time there was a break in the gale, the captain tried to punch his way out, but the powerful wind and waves forced him back into port.

Captain McKay saw his break on Thursday evening November 15th. The gale seemed to moderate and at 8:40 p.m. he headed for Ontonagon, about 75 miles to the east. Once he unloaded passengers and freight he would continue on for Portage. At 10:00 p.m. two other weather bound steamers, the *City of Duluth* and *China* followed the *Manistee's* lead. Both were headed directly for Portage, approximately 40 miles beyond Ontonagon. When the *Manistee*

A commemorative postcard of the Manistee *after the loss. It is believed the captain is on the right and chief engineer on the left.* Author

Went Missing Redux

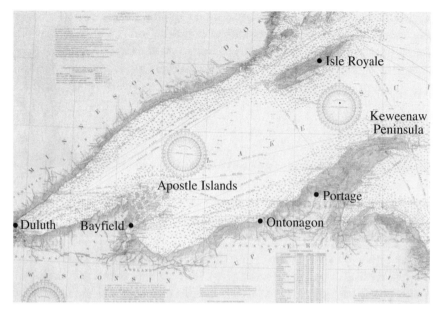

left she was light several passengers who transferred to the larger *City of Duluth*. Whether it was motivated by a strange premonition or just the desire for better quarters or a quicker trip since they were going directly to Portage isn't known.[iv]

When the *City of Duluth* and *China* arrived at Portage both captains routinely reported the *Manistee's* departure but since she was stopping at Ontonagon her arrival would obviously be delayed. When she still didn't turn up it was thought she likely returned to Duluth for more freight.

Real concern only set in on Monday when word came from Ontonagon that the *Manistee* never arrived at all and no one there had any idea where she could be. What happened to the *Manistee*?

Monday night November 19, the tug *Maythem* steamed out of Portage searching for the missing steamer. After checking at Ontonagon she ran north by half east for 35 miles where she located a small field of floating wreckage. It included half the aft portion of the port side of the *Manistee's* Texas, a wooden bucket and some charcoal. The tug ran for another ten miles but found nothing more… just an empty lake. Considering the situation the captain concluded any more wreckage would be to the southeast of his position but as the weather was starting to kick up, he returned to port.[v]

On Wednesday November 21 the tug searched again, running from Isle Royale's Siskiwit Bay to Washington Harbor, to the north shore of Minnesota at Pigeon River, west to a point opposite Outer Island and west across the south shore to Portage. In addition, the tug *Boutin* was looking to the

Lost Off The Keweenaw - The Manistee

northeast 45 miles from Outer Island and then returning and cruising through the Apostles to Oronto Bay and past the Porcupine Mountains. Port Arthur authorities were also telegraphed to ask incoming ships if they saw anything of the missing *Manistee*.[vi]

The tugs found nothing however other ships did come across evidence of disaster bobbing silently in the cold gray waves. On November 25 the Ward Line steamer *Oscela* discovered *Manistee* wreckage floating around in heavy seas east of the Apostle Islands. The day prior the tug SWAIN running from Duluth with a tow steamed through a big field about four hours out of Copper Harbor. Chairs, tables, beds, barrels, buckets, bed clothing, mattresses and various foodstuffs all bore mute testimony to the demise of the steamer.

Wreckage from the *Manistee* continued to wash ashore on the Keweenaw Peninsula for six months, a constant reminder of loss. Some of the flotsam even reached the Canadian shore. In a grim reminder of the ship that never arrived wreckage appeared on the Ontonagon beaches too.

The steamer's rudder and a huge amount of barreled flour came ashore near Eagle Harbor and Copper Harbor. Copper Harbor Range Lightkeeper William Tresisc alone hauled 44 barrels from the lake. The long-suffering Keweenaw Peninsula residents knew a good thing when they saw it and as soon as anything of value was recovered, it was stolen. This larceny greatly irritated the *Manistee's* agent, sent to the area to salvage whatever cargo he possibly could. He was on a doomed mission, a lone honest man in countryside of thieves!

The Manistee *was a typical Great Lakes propeller. Author*

The Manistee *fast in the ice. Note the spread eagle above the turret pilothouse and prominent arches. Author*

Manistee wreckage was strewn over the Keweenaw beaches. Several oars, a piece of signboard carrying the letters "MANIS," a yawl boat, a barrel filled with eggs, a keg of whisky and an intact passenger's trunk filled with clothing and even a silver watch, all found their way ashore. The mast came up on the peninsula's Sand Bay and companionway at Ontonagon. The propeller *City of Fremont* reported the large wooden gold painted eagle from above the pilothouse roof and wheel ended up at Union Bay along with 20 barrels of flour. The fact the wheel was lashed hard over indicated an attempt to leave her had been made. Lashing down the wheel would serve to keep her moving in a given direction, freeing the helmsman to abandon ship too!

The *City of Fremont* took the place of the *Manistee* on the south shore route. Described as a "very pretty boat," and one of the fasted on the lake, the *Ashland Press* claimed it would soon be very popular with the traveling public.[vii]

Lost Off The Keweenaw - The **Manistee**

It was also the *City of Fremont* that delivered the first news of the *Manistee* loss to the folks at Eagle Harbor. When she came in on November 21, all of her flags were at half-mast. Once locals asked why, the report of the disaster was electrifying![viii]

In June wreckage thought to be from the *Manistee* was discovered ashore at Whitefish Point at the extreme east end of the lake. It consisted of a box with a number of photos, a parasol and marriage certificate dated 1876 for one William Heighes of Calumet and Miss Victoria L. Masters of St. Clair.[ix]

The following August part of the cabin, several life preservers, a water barrel rack and several smaller items were discovered on Point Mamainse on the north shore of the lake. Just yards away was the skeleton of a man clad in a badly decayed fur-trimmed coat. Was he from the *Manistee* or just the victim of storm, crime or circumstance? If he was from the steamer, his was the only body reportedly ever recovered. Some wreckage was also found on Caribou Island, far in the east northeast part of the lake.

The sudden and inexplicable loss of the *Manistee* caused a profound sensation in the Lake Superior maritime community. No one could comprehend how a staunch, well-built (and recently rebuilt) vessel commanded by an experienced captain, on a regular run, founder. The loss becomes more confusing when it is realized the steamers *China* and *City of Duluth* were a bare hour and twenty minutes behind her, a distance of perhaps 10 miles and they steamed through the same gale without mishap.[x]

What happened to the *Manistee?*

The gale was certainly a real "gagger" as the old sailors would say. The *Marquette Mining Journal* on November 17 reported the storm was, "one of unexpected violence" and that a "large number of vessels sheltered in Marquette." Considering that Captain McKay decided to shelter in Bayfield instead of keeping strictly to his schedule is testimony to his concern. As soon as the gale showed any sign of moderating, McKay, though, continued on his run. Ships don't make money by waiting around in port every time the lake gets "wavy." Since the *China* and *City of Duluth* quickly followed, it is clear the other captains agreed with McKay's weather sense.

The best guess of the *Manistee's* fate was she was overwhelmed by a sudden and intense local squall. The further eastward she steamed, the further she was from the shelter of land. Once she cleared the tip of Outer Island, the most northern of the Apostles, the seas would have built up over 60 miles before striking her.

Steaming for Ontonagon, the *Manistee* would have taken the seas on her port beam. In Mansfield's classic *History of the Great Lakes*, the report of the steamer's loss said she was struck by a sudden southwest gale. A quick wind shift from the northwest to southwest would not be unusual in the prevailing conditions. A powerful squall could have knocked her over on her beam ends, a position from which she could never recover. Such a freak squall would also explain why the *China* and *City of Duluth* were not affected and reached Portage without incident.[xi]

According to the official journal of the Light Station at Eagle Harbor, the gale blew from the 11th through the 15th and on the 15th it kept "shifting from point to point."

Central to the sudden squall theory is the idea she was a sound vessel just caught in the wrong place at the wrong time. There is another theory, however, that the steamer had become rotten over the years and was in poor condition to face a strong gale. If true, the *Manistee's* life span in the storm would have been very short, making her unable to stand up to the stress of wind and wave. However since she was rebuilt in 1879 with additional work in 1881 this would seem unlikely.

There is no direct evidence for the rotten theory. Following the loss the *Saginaw News* editorialized the *Manistee*, "should have been retired from service long before." It further claimed one of their reporters had traveled on her the year prior and, "found not only that our suspicions were correct but that people who had known her for years were in the expectation of her collapse constantly" and that, "someone blundered by allowing passengers aboard." Such condemnation was not universal. The editors of the *Marquette Mining Journal* disagreed with the *Saginaw News*, stating there was entirely too much hindsight in their observations.[xii] I concur.

An expert mariner arguing against a "rotten" ship theory was Captain Eber Ward, manager of the well-respected Ward Line. He took a trip on the *Manistee* running her entire route in the fall of 1882 and found no deficiencies in either the steamer or her captain. Ward later stated, "his service while in the employ of the writer was marked with great success, combining rare good judgment and skilled seamanship with remarkable prudence and at all times having in mind the interests of his boat and passengers and their safety as the first and last consideration."[xiii]

So what can we surmise from the mystery of the *Manistee* loss?

The fact she was rebuilt only shortly before the loss isn't conclusive proof she was rotten. She was undoubtedly rebuilt because she needed it, which in a wooden vessel is common. Could the yard have done a bad job of the rebuild, perhaps missing critical rotten timbers and thus not giving her the strength expected? In the stress of a gale those same timbers lacked the strength to hold the ship together. While the theory she had major structural problems because of rotten timbers is in my opinion without merit, it is possible critical hull timbers could have been missed. You can't prove what didn't happen.

The lack of bodies speaks volumes for how fast the end came. Had she sank slowly some folks could have made it to a lifeboat or even climbed aboard the Texas deck when it broke off. The most likely explanation for the missing bodies was many people were caught below decks and trapped when she suddenly rolled and dove for the bottom. Considering the fury of the mounting waves it would have been far more comfortable for the passengers to stay safe below decks or in their cabins.

The location of the Texas deck is the most important clue to where she sank. Small stuff like buckets and deck cargo wash overboard all the time but a steamer usually loses her Texas only when she is sinking and air pressure inside is sufficient to literally blow it off. The tug located the Texas three days after the ship's estimated date of loss and in a location about right for a vessel on course from Bayfield to Ontonagon, considering a generally southwest gale.

The failure of the tugs to find any other clues to the *Manistee's* disappearance shouldn't be considered overly important. Searching the lake for wreckage is never an easy job. There is a tremendous amount of water to cover and a wreckage field is usually fairly small, regardless of the size of the lost ship. Add in a rough sea and the task can be well neigh impossible, the results determined by luck more than skill. It was also five days before any major searching was done and five more before a significant effort started. Much can happen in that period. Vital clues waiting for discovery could have been lost forever.

Real evidence of the exact location of the *Manistee* foundering is nearly nonexistent. With the exception of the wreckage found by the *Maythem* and that located on the Keweenaw near Ontonagon, there weren't any significant clues. That said there certainly was no evidence she struck Superior Shoal as one wild theory claimed.[xiv]

In May of 1885 a bottle with a message purporting to come from the *Manistee* was discovered by a local resident, Augustus Archambeau, floating near Fish Creek at the head of Wisconsin's Ashland Bay. The cryptic note said, "This is of the *Manistee*, in a fearful storm. May not live to see morning. Ever yours to the world. John McKay, Capt." The agent for the Wisconsin Central Railroad and the Collector for the Port of Ashland, two local marine men familiar with McKay's signature and writing, pronounced it a genuine last message from a dying ship. However, Captain George McKay, Captain John McKay's brother, considered it a hoax. He reasoned that as the gale on the night of the steamer's loss was southwest, it should have driven the bottle northeast and toward the north shore, not into Ashland Bay. His opinion was it was the bad joke of someone trying to cause a sensation and not from his lost brother.

There is a story of another note too. In May 1897 James Taggart, a Bayfield lumberman reportedly found a bottle embedded in the sand of Chequamagon Bay with a note nearly too faded to read: "November 1883, Left Bayfield at 1:10 p.m. just in sight of Michigan Lighthouse. We may not survive this storm. Heavily laden and hard to turn in the storm." The glass of the bottle was said to be very worn from rolling around in the sand adding credibility to it's purported age.[xv]

There is a long tradition of messages in bottles from Great Lakes wrecks. Some were undoubtedly authentic and others fake. The verdict is still out whether either or both of the *Manistee* messages were false or true. Regardless neither shed any light on the cause of loss or location.

Besides Captain McKay, George L. Steaton was the clerk, P. Cullen engineer and Andrew Mack first mate. Rounding out the crew were two cooks, two to three waiters, a female chambermaid, firemen and 15 deckhands, totaling a crew of about 25. The exact number may never be known.

The death of John McKay was the real shocker. He was very highly regarded in the maritime world and his loss was both surprising and appalling. He started sailing when still a teenager with his father on a schooner and even wheeled for a year on the propeller *Iron City*. By age 17 he was second mate on the propeller *General Taylor* and his brother George, six years older, was captain. In 1861 he transferred with George to the propeller *Mineral Rock* with George as captain and John first mate. When the *Pewabic* came out in 1863 the pair moved to her. In 1864 John took over the propeller *Dubuque*, later moving to the *St. Paul* and the *Norman* before finally taking the *Manistee* in 1873. Nearly all of his time was on Lake Superior, so he was intimately familiar with the many moods and challenges of the big lake. George was cursed to command the *Pewabic* when she collided with the propeller *Meteor* off Alpena in Lake Huron in August 1865. Between 75 - 100 people perished in the disaster. The weather was perfect and it was believed both vessels were running close aboard to pass messages when they smashed into each other.

Following the *Manistee* loss an old friend described John as, "a sailor born. He was a part of his ship always, as much as any timber in her. He was always at his post, never letting anything stand between him and his duty to his boat and employers. He was kind hearted and generous to a fault, loved his friends and was forgiving to those who trespassed against him. He was a man, every

Lost Off The Keweenaw - The Manistee

inch of him."[xvi] While this is obviously more a eulogy than a critical appraisal of Captain McKay's seamanship, it none-the-less does paint an illuminating picture of a competent and well-respected Great Lakes navigator.

The two brothers, John and George were very close. It was said even months after the wreck George cried like a baby when discussing the shipwreck.

Ashland fish dealer Alphonse LeBel provided a truly bizarre twist to the wreck. He claimed one of his fishermen caught a big lake trout in November 1889 and when it was gutted, a silver spoon engraved *Manistee* tumbled out of it's stomach!

Of course no ship can sink without tales of treasure and the *Manistee* is no different. There was a rumor she carried 199 tons of copper plus gold and silver in her strongbox. That there is no proof of such a claim doesn't dissuade "true believers."

Questions, Always Questions - The *W.H. Gilcher*

Technology is the key to progress. Those folks that eschew it invariably fail. But when applied without full understanding and development, it can prove disastrous.

In the beginning of European navigation on the Great Lakes ships were built of wood as elsewhere. It was strong, resilient, relatively inexpensive and generally available. If well maintained, a good wood ship could last thirty years or more.

It didn't take shipbuilders long to recognize the inherent value of iron. It was stronger and would last far longer than wood. A number of big iron bulk freighters soon rumbled down the ways the first being the 287-foot *Onoko* from the Globe Iron Works in 1882. She worked the ore trade for 33 years before sinking in western Lake Superior in 1915 after she began dropping bottom plates. Marine men thought an earlier grounding likely damaged the bottom more than realized. From a ship owners viewpoint there was nothing wrong with iron as such but it was expensive compared to wood.

Iron had been used on the Great Lakes before the *Onoko*. The first substantial iron passenger/freight ship was the *Merchant* built in Buffalo in 1862. Doubtless her construction was partially at least driven by the Civil War induced shipping boom. The first iron ship on the lakes was the U.S. Navy gunboat *Michigan* assembled at Erie, Pennsylvania in 1844 from plate rolled at Pittsburgh. She was also the first iron vessel built for the Navy.

Steel of course was considered better than iron but more expensive and initially it was restricted to special applications only. When new manufacturing processes were developed steel making became easier and cheaper. With the

The Onoko was the first iron freighter built on the lakes. Author

greater availability and a cost less than iron, it became the material of choice and shipbuilders quickly adapted to it. Iron was also thought to be more brittle than steel, an important consideration for the Great Lakes where vessel flexing in a shorter wave period was vital. Expensive new machinery was designed, built and installed in shipyards, ready for the rush of new orders for steel boats.[i]

The first steel bulk freighter was the 324-foot *Spokane*, also built by the Globe Iron Works in 1886.[ii] The *Spokane* was originally designed as an iron vessel but when the owner discovered building her from steel only cost

Questions, Always Questions - The W.H. Gilcher

The first iron-hulled propeller on the Upper Lakes was the 200-foot Merchant *built in 1862. Author*

$10,000 more, steel it would be. Engineers calculated she was also as much as 29% stronger than iron due to the substitution.[iii] More steel ships soon followed. In 1890 the Cleveland Shipbuilding Company launched four big steel freighters. Two, the nearly identical *Western Reserve* and the *W.H. Gilcher* were remarkably successful, at least up until their foundering. Both competed for bulk cargo carrying records with each other. It was a case of "one upsmanship." In fact the *Gilcher* grabbed the grain record quickly by hauling a staggering 113,885 bushels of wheat from Chicago to Buffalo in a single trip.[iv]

On August 30, 1892 the 301-foot, 2329 gross ton *Western Reserve* was upbound on Lake Superior from Cleveland for

The Michigan *was the first iron gunboat built for the U.S. Navy and was based out of Erie. Author*

The Spokane *was the first steel bulk freighter on the lakes.* Author

Two-Harbors, Minnesota. Running light, (without cargo) she intended to load iron ore for the trip down. A summer gale was lashing the lake but the ship was not experiencing any trouble. As the old time sailors used to say, "she was going along like an old shoe."

About 60 miles above Whitefish Point she achieved the buoyancy of a rock and plummeted to the bottom of the lake. The popular theory is she broke in two in the vicinity of the number one hatch forward, the disaster occurring about 9:00 p.m. Regardless of the wrecking mechanics, there wasn't any warning at all. One minute the bow and stern were in the right places and the next they were rapidly sinking! The crew and passengers took to the boats one of which immediately overturned in the waves drowning

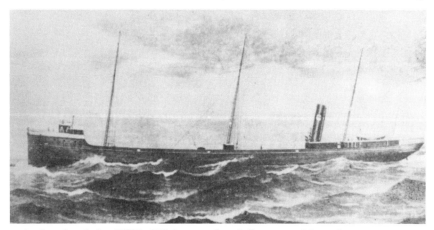

A sketch of the W.H. Gilcher *under full steam. Note the carry-over masts.* Author

Questions, Always Questions - The W.H. Gilcher

The Western Reserve *loss in 1892 cast doubt on her steel construction. Author*

those aboard. The second reached the breakers off the lonely Michigan shore only to capsize in the crashing surf. Only wheelsman Harry Stewart, managed to stagger to shore alive. He was the sole survivor.

An especially tragic aspect of the wreck was the death of the managing owner Captain Peter G. Minch, his wife Anna and two of their seven children, Charles age 10 and Florence age 9, together with his wife's younger sister and her nine year old daughter. It was intended to be a pleasant vacation trip for the family. Doubtless Captain Minch also thought it was a good way to introduce his son to the shipping business. Peter took over from his father and likely his son would follow in his footsteps. It was not to be. A total of 26 people died in the wreck and it was only wheelsman Stewart's testimony providing any insight to what happened.[v]

Some marine men doubted Stewart's explanation skeptical he really saw a crack in the hull given the gale and darkness. After all he claimed he was asleep in his cabin when the break occurred as opposed to being on the bridge. In addition the fracture should have snapped the steering chains causing the ship to come around in the northwest seas rather than stay on course as he supposedly claimed. Stewart also never mentioned any sagging, which should have been significant had the *Western Reserve* broken in two. Given the confusion caused by the night, gale and shipwreck, did he really see what he claimed?[vi]

But without other evidence to review marine men were forced to accept Stewart's report. At the time of the disaster she was driving hard into the gale without water ballast in her forward compartments. It was thought this lack of "stiffening" may have played a role. There were also claims she was pushing too hard to keep a schedule rather than accept a weather delay and ease off in the gale.[vii]

Being the sole survivor of the wreck didn't keep Harry Stewart down. He later went on to a long sailing career including captaining the *Onoko* in 1910 continuing his relationship with "new" ships.[viii]

An exhaustive investigation was unable to directly fix the cause of loss. The ship's plans and specifications were carefully examined but they provided no clues as to the cause of such a cataclysmic structural failure. It took the loss of another vessel to bring a proximate cause into sharper focus. Legendary naval architect Frank E. Kirby looked over the plans of the *Western Reserve* carefully searching for a design flaw. He found none and concluded the plans called for, "...ample material in fact superior to most ships."[ix]

The *W.H. Gilcher* was launched on December 18, 1890 at the same Cleveland Shipbuilding Company yard where a mere four months earlier the *Western Reserve* slid down the ways. Reputedly the *Gilcher* was the largest ship ever built in the city to that date. The new steamer was 301.5 feet in length, 41.2 feet in beam and 21.1 feet in depth. She was powered by a 1,400 horsepower triple expansion steam engine also built by the Cleveland Shipbuilding Company.[x]

The Minch family was deeply involved in Great Lakes shipping. Philip J. Minch, Peter G.'s father was born in Germany, immigrating to America in 1840. Originally a shoemaker, he settled in Vermilion, Ohio and for a time cobbled away on his last. After marrying a local girl, Anna C. Leimbach, he decided to build ships starting with a simple scow and as the business proved profitable, built and managed bigger and bigger ships. In 1887 he moved his family to Cleveland to better manage the expanding fleet but died the same year. Anna bore him eight children, four dying before age six. One of the vessels he held a financial interest in was the *Onoko*, demonstrating his vision of the future.

Philip's son Peter G. followed in his father's wake going to sea at age 14 during the summer and attending Oberlin College during the fall and winter. Fleet owners needed business skills as well as sailing proficiency.

Philip's daughter Sophia not only had a famous schooner named after her, the *Sophia Minch*, but also married a real estate broker named Henry Steinbrenner who lived on the same street as the Minch family, Kinsman Street.

Questions, Always Questions - The W.H. Gilcher

Philip J.s wife Anna C. proved to be a woman of strong stuff. When he died unexpectedly she assumed control of the Minch Company running it until 1901. Given the times, a woman heading up a major business was extremely unusual. In 1905 her son in law Henry (Steinbrenner, married to Sophia) reorganized the company into the Kinsman Transportation Company the name coming from the street both families lived on. Henry and Sophia produced George M. who became a naval architect and eventually fathered the present George M. Steinbrenner III, of New York Yankees fame.[xi]

The steamer *Anna C. Minch* was named after Anna but suffered the misfortune of sinking with all 24 hands south of Pentwater, Michigan, Lake Michigan in the infamous 1940 Armistice Day storm.[xii]

The relationships between Minch, Steinbrenner, *Onoko*, *Western Reserve* and *W.H. Gilcher* are complicated but fascinating, especially when viewed in the overall contest of Great Lakes maritime history. Key to the relationship is the American Shipbuilding Company.

The company was incorporated in New Jersey in 1899, a state offering major tax advantages at the time. The new company was formed by the consolidation of three major Cleveland firms, the Cleveland Shipbuilding Company, Ship Owners Dry Dock Company and the Globe Iron Works plus five other smaller concerns. Globe built the *Onoko* in which Peter J. Minch had a financial interest. The Cleveland Ship Building Company designed and built the *Western Reserve* and *W. H. Gilcher*. In 1952 George M. Steinbrenner III (Yankees' fame) led a group of investors in a takeover of the firm. At the time he was the owner of Kinsman Transportation, the old Minch company. Small world isn't it?[xiii]

The end for the *Gilcher* came on Friday, October 8, 1892. It followed the inexplicable loss of the *Western Reserve* by a scant two months. At 2:20 p.m. the *Gilcher* passed through the Straits of Mackinac bound from Buffalo to Milwaukee with a cargo of 3200 tons of hard coal. The captain of a schooner observing her noted she was "laboring hard with wind and wave." There is some mistaken thought she could have run through the Manitou Passage, a popular shipping route for traffic wishing to cut the corner in northern Lake Michigan. It's a path marked on both east and west by dangerous shoals and reefs but for a vessel on course, represents no danger. In fact she ran northwest of the Manitou Islands, far outside the Passage. Twenty-one men were in the crew. [xiv]

After the *Gilcher* was lost Captain Samuel Dodd of the White Shoal Lightship said he saw the *Gilcher* steaming past him about 2:00 p.m. in the afternoon and heading for the northern passage around the Beaver Island group prior to turning south for Milwaukee. Since the wind was blowing

WENT MISSING REDUX

northwest the steamer was in relatively protected waters thus the lightship captain saw no reason to think she broke up and sank.

The gale considerably disrupted shipping in northern Lake Michigan. On October 29 the North Manitou Island Life-Saving Station crew discovered the small schooner *Maggie Thompson* of Milwaukee ashore on the island. The Life-Savers were on the beach the entire night rendering assistance. The next day they helped the steamer *Pawnee* look for her two barges lost in the storm. Storm and gale always meant work for the Life-Saving Service.[xv]

A rolling gale was blowing but like the *Western Reserve*, most mariners thought it was of no extraordinary consequence. Smaller ships were knocked about but big freighters like the *Gilcher* would continue on their schedules. Many observers felt the gale peaked in late afternoon or early evening.

The *Gilcher* was under the command of Captain Leeds H. Weeks from Vermilion, Ohio, a mariner of long experience and ability.[xvi] The majority of his crew also hailed from the same environs. Based on the Minch relationship with Vermilion it is worth speculating if preference was given to local men? The chance to work on a bright new steamer like the *Gilcher* was one to be grabbed at and getting a crew wasn't hard for a new "super" ship. Weeks brought the *Gilcher* out of the yard and continued to master her until her sinking. But something unexpected happened that night in northern Lake Michigan. Regardless of his implicit confidence in his ship she never finished her trip to Milwaukee. The lake just swallowed her up!^{xvii}

At first the general location of loss was thought to be somewhere off High Island in northern Lake Michigan. It was where Captain Stuffelbaum of the schooner *Hattie B. Perene* spotted some of the steamer's wreckage, including lifeboat strongbacks. One of the strongbacks looked like it was cut with an axe, giving the impression a crewman tried to launch her very quickly and in desperation.[xviii]

Much more wreckage was found about 40 miles south of High Island near North Manitou Island by the steamer *White and Friant*. One of the odd pieces picked up was a piece of cabin work with "James Riley 9 PM" carved on it. The steamer *Pawnee* also discovered a field in the same area consisting of miscellaneous furniture, stanchions and bedding. However there was uncertainty that it was from the missing steamer. Captain Peter Olsen and his North Manitou Island Life-Saving Service crew recovered more wreckage while patrolling the beaches including broken hatch covers. Some was clearly marked W.H. Gilcher. Judging from the wreckage, the position of the wreck was generally fixed as west of the island and near the downbound shipping lane.[xix]

Later reports came in from vessels in the area during the gale. The captain of the schooner *Waukesha* said he followed a steamer's lights until they

Questions, Always Questions - The W.H. Gilcher

suddenly disappeared near South Fox Island. Did she dive for the bottom at that moment or just dropped from sight? Was it the *Gilcher* at all?

Vesselmen were unable to determine the reason for the loss of the big and nearly new freighter. Unlike the *Western Reserve*, nobody survived to tell the tale. But the cause couldn't have been the gale. The old wooden steamers *Eddy* and *Albany* were in the same area and while they reported it was a real "snorter," both came through without problem. Why didn't the much bigger, newer and supposedly stronger *Gilcher* survive?

Some mariners thought she sank as the result of a collision with the 279-ton, 130-foot schooner *Ostrich*. The schooner with her crew of six men and a woman cook also disappeared in the gale. Owned and mastered by John McKay, she was bound from Milwaukee to Torch Lake for lumber. The

Could a schooner have smashed into the big Gilcher *and actually sunk her? Author*

WENT MISSING REDUX

likelihood of collision seemed more certain when wreckage, thought to be from the schooner, washed ashore at North Manitou Island intermingled with the *Gilcher* debris.[xx] This has an eerie similarity to the *D.A. Wells - Alpena* collision speculation. But a schooner foundering in a gale wasn't unusual, so the connection with the *Gilcher* loss isn't rock solid.

The *Gilcher* was an insurance loss of $180,000, the *Ostrich* about $8,000. None of the bodies of the schooner and few from the steamer were ever reported recovered.

The second engineer on the *Gilcher* was 35-year old Thomas Finley. His only brother John was also an engineer, sailing on the steamer *Northwind* of the Northern Steamship Company. In fact when the *Gilcher* foundered the *Northwind* was perhaps only 30 miles distant but brother John never learned about the disaster until his ship reached port in Buffalo.

He immediately left the *Northwind* and took a train at midnight from Buffalo for the vicinity of the wreck, arriving about four o'clock in the afternoon of the following day. The North Manitou Island Life-Saving Station crew took him out to the island where he examined some of the upper works of the *Gilcher* and quantities of other wreckage on shore. He also saw the fifteen life preservers with the straps broken and the bodies of the steward Greene and a fireman named Williams. The bodies came ashore wearing preservers. The remains of another crewmember was so black with deterioration he was not even recognizable. According to the newspapers it was later buried on the island although there is no official record of the interment. Locally burying the bodies of shipwreck victims that were found wasn't unusual during this period especially when neither identification could be made or next of kin located.

Finley discovered another clue to the wreck, learning that Charles Rowe of Harbor Springs, Michigan, while sailing in the vicinity of the wreck, picked up the *Gilcher's* midship spar about twelve miles northeast from South Fox Island light and towed it to the island. Examining it he saw it was split, undoubtedly he felt because the vessel broke in two before sinking. The spar was held together by the stays (standing rigging) before the stress of the breakup split it. Further evidence of the ship breaking in two came from the center of the number 6 hatch cover. When found on the beach it was broken across the middle. Was the fracture the result of the actual cracking of the ship or as the result of more conventional sinking? All told, Finley spent about fifteen days in the hopeless search for his brother's remains before finally abandoning all hope. Thomas Finely's body was never recovered.

Before leaving, however, John Finley learned another piece of startling information. It seems about twenty-four hours before the loss of the *Gilcher*

Questions, Always Questions - The **W.H. Gilcher**

captain Buchanan of the small schooner *Seamen* claimed to have seen her 20 miles northwest of North Manitou and 15 miles west of South Fox Island around 8:00 p.m. He later related, "We sighted a big steamer in front of us. We had the right of way and burned our torch for the steamer to make room for us but she did not make the slightest move to do so. She lay with her head west-northwest, directly into the wind and did not seem to be working her wheel any more than to keep pointed into the wind." No one was visible on deck either.[xxi] Did this mean the *Gilcher* was disabled? Or was she starting to break up and the captain gathered his men below to plan their abandonment of her? Or had they left her already, thus explaining the lack of crew on deck? If so why weren't the lifeboats found regardless of the survival of the crew or not?

Later in the year, apparently in December, Thomas Finley's wife also went to North Manitou Island to search for his body. Accompanying her was Mrs. M.J. Zinysfer, a reputed clairvoyant, "doctress" and "life reader" from Buffalo. Perhaps help "from the other side" would aid her in finding her husband. Apparently the "other side" was otherwise occupied and she returned home without finding him.[xxii]

Later shipping experts began to put one and one together with most distressing results. They reluctantly concluded the reasons for the loss of both the *Western Reserve* and *W.H. Gilcher* were brittle steel fractures.

Driven by the loss of the *Gilcher* navel architects began to ask serious questions concerning the quality of the steel used in vessels. The steel should have met very exacting standards and samples routinely tested to assure consistent quality. This didn't happen.

Naval architect Fred A. Ballin of the Detroit Boat Works explained the problem saying it was, "...almost impossible to get a homogeneous stock of steel even in the same plate. We had lab tests made and found that the plates and angles would crack in handling, heating or punching." He also said that considerable money could be saved in using Bessemer steel but the steel was unfit for shipbuilding. The preferred steel was that made by the open hearth or electric furnace methods. Particular attention is paid to the metallurgical properties of the steel, to control it's ability to withstand the strain of a flexing and pounding vessel.

The faulty steel theories held that both ships developed small cracks and fractures in their hulls and supporting frames. Since the *Western Reserve* was running light, without ballast, a condition when stress on the vessel can be the highest, it was believed she snapped under the excessive strain brought on by the gale. The cracks were not anticipated since the ship was so new and steel so much superior to iron. However there was an important difference between the two ships. The *Western Reserve* was running light, without cargo, thus considered more vulnerable to fracture. But the *Gilcher's* holds were filled with coal thus was "stiffer" and less likely to crack. Or so the theory went.

It is not unusual for cracks to develop in a steel vessel. Generally they are small and early detection results in simple repair. There are exceptions worth noting. In November 1958 the 623-foot bulk freighter *Carl D. Bradley* sank in a Lake Michigan gale under similar circumstances, breaking in two during the height of a storm. The 568-foot *Daniel J. Morrell* broke in a Lake Huron gale in November 1966. The *Bradley* took down all but two of her crew and *Morrell* every man but one. When the *Edward Y. Townsend*, following the *Morrell* up Lake Huron, was examined at the Soo directly on her arrival there, Coast Guard inspectors found a large crack running across her spar deck. She was immediately retired never to sail again. Later when being towed to Spain for scrapping, she snapped in two and sank about 400 miles south of Newfoundland.

It is important to realize a big steel vessel is not inanimate in a seaway. The ship is in a sense alive, twisting and heaving as she battles the seas. This movement places tremendous strain on the structure. Yet if a ship remains immobile, the strains are far greater. The designers must consider the effect of these powerful forces and build the ship to withstand them. It wasn't unusual for hull rivets to "pop" and literally explode off the hull like bullets during the stress of a Great Lakes gale. Following the infamous 1940 Armistice Day storm several ships that survived the blow went immediately into drydock for repair where workers found hundreds, perhaps even thousands of "popped" rivet heads laying in the holds.

One of the steamer's owners, J.C. Gilcher, believed she hit an unknown shoal near South Fox Island or collided with another vessel, stating, "…she could not have broken in two… I don't believe that weather alone could have overcome her."[xxiii]

Regardless of Gilcher's belief, marine men generally thought it was unlikely the *Gilcher* struck a shoal and subsequently broke up since there was comparatively little wreckage. A ship hard on a reef would have been swept clean by the waves. Literally everything above decks would have been washed off, including the two buoyant metal lifeboats, which were never found. Following the loss the shipping lane was checked for any unknown obstructions, something they may have missed in earlier surveys, but nothing was found.

The idea of the *Gilcher* sinking after colliding with a wooden schooner like the *Ostrich* is also unlikely. The big steel steamer would have sliced the wooden ship in two and should not have suffered major damage herself. Even

Questions, Always Questions - The W.H. Gilcher

if mortally wounded, there should have been time to launch lifeboats. The *Gilcher* would not have immediately plunged to the bottom.

Perhaps the most important clue to the *Gilcher* disappearance lies with her lifeboats. Since they were never found it could be surmised they are still shackled to her when she sank - this despite the believed attempt to clear at least one set of strongbacks with an axe. The boats still being shackled meant the ship sank very quickly, in mere minutes. Such a rapid sinking could only be caused by a cataclysmic event, such as a structural failure, in effect breaking in two. Any sinking by schooner collision would have been much slower with time to abandon ship.

Of course all of the theories concerning the *Gilcher* are exactly that - theories. No one knows what really happened. All that remains are questions, always questions.

One immediate result of the *Gilcher* loss was a dramatic increase in lake insurance rates. The *Western Reserve* could have been a fluke, a one of a kind accident, but when the *Gilcher* pulled the same trick it was time to take a very close look at the new steel boats. After all, the *Gilcher* was the largest single loss in lake insurance to that date. Contracts to build new steel boats literally evaporated with considerable expense to the yards that had invested in new tooling and machinery for the latest steel technology.

Superstition always played a role in sailor culture and the *Gilcher* was no different. Old salts remember the shipyard launched her without a name assigned, never a good way to start a lucky carrier.[xxiv]

The wreck remains missing, resting deep in Lake Michigan. There is a rumor that on July 12, 1935 Chicago hardhat diver Frank Blair located the hull but at best it is only a tale.[xxv]

Modern searches have failed to unlock the mystery of the *Gilcher*. She is there somewhere, hiding on the bottom of Lake Michigan.

ADDENDUM TO CRACKING - *GILCHER*

The problem of vessels breaking in two is most typified by the famous World War II Liberty ships. Between 1941 and 1945 eighteen American shipyards produced 2,751 Liberties, easily the largest number of ships produced to a single design. Considering the tremendous carnage in the North Atlantic due to German submarine attacks on merchant vessel convoys, the need for replacement hulls was critical. Certainly construction standards were compromised in comparison with peacetime construction. And it must be remembered ship design life was a mere five years!

Went Missing Redux

A typical Liberty ship. US Navy

Liberties were built using welded sections that were in turn welded together as opposed to the more traditional riveting. Ships constructed with rivets normally took several months to build. Welding was much faster. Finding a skilled workforce proved to be a problem not dissimilar to that Canadian Car faced building the minesweepers in Fort William (see *Inkermann* and *Cerisoles*). Experienced shipyard workers were either in military service or already committed to other construction. To fill the void an army of untrained and unskilled employees was recruited. Training was generally done "on the job" with mixed results. Many of the new workers were women leading to the term "Rosie the Riveter."

The first of the class took 244 days to complete which, as experience was gained, dropped to 42 days. The record was an astounding four days, 15-1/2 hours prior to launching! This was of course a publicity stunt and a great deal of fitting out was still required. Regardless, the speed of construction was incredible.

Early Liberties suffered hull and deck cracks resulting in some being lost catastrophically. During the war roughly 1,500 instances of brittle steel fractures were reported. Nineteen ships broke in half without warning, one while moored to her Boston dock. Initially it was thought the cracking was related to welding but later detailed analysis proved it was caused by the grade of steel used, which was prone to embrittlement. Water temperature also played a role. Liberties running the cold North Atlantic were exposed to temperatures that could fall below a critical point when the mechanism of cracking altered from ductile the hull could fracture relatively easily. By contrast none of the Liberties running in the warmer Pacific reportedly cracked.

Welding did play a secondary role however. Welded ships, as opposed to riveted ones, allow cracks to run for long distances while on a riveted ship the crack will be "caught" in a rivet joint or at the next hull plate. With welded construction, the ship's hull was in theory one single plate. Once the crack started to run it only stopped when it ran out of steel. On a riveted hull it typically ran no more than 20 feet. A common place for hull cracks to start was at a square hatch corner coinciding with a welded seam. The corner and weld tended to act as stress concentrators. The predominantly welded (as opposed to riveted) hull construction then allowed cracks to run for large distances unimpeded. In one instance the crack completely circled the ship. Overloading a ship or under storm stress increased the potential for cracking.

Once the problem was recognized the Liberties were reinforced with additional bracing mitigating the problem.

Some experts also blame the problem of cracking steel for the *Titanic* loss in April 1912. The theory being while she collided with the iceberg, it was the resulting fracturing of her steel hull due to the particular qualities of the material and coldwater environment that really sank her.

The *Titanic* was constructed with the standard carbon steel used for period marine construction, which tended to have higher levels of sulfur and phosphorus, and insufficient manganese to mitigate the effects of sulfur. As a result, the steel was much more brittle at lower temperatures. A detailed analysis of steel samples from the *Titanic* by the National Institute of Standards and Technology (U.S. Department of Commerce) also showed great variability of properties between different steel plates showing a lack of quality control during manufacture.

A cracked hull on a Liberty ship. Such a crack could be catastrophic. US Navy

WENT MISSING REDUX

Given the state of knowledge available to engineers when the *Titanic* was built no error can be attributed to them.

There is another variation to consider too. In the case of the *Titanic* there appears to be crack propagation along the rivet holes. During her construction as well as other *Olympic* - class ships, the rivet holes were cold punched through the steel plates before riveting the plates to the framing. This method creates micro-cracks around the edges of the rivet holes. In addition, many of the *Titanic's* rivets were hydraulically driven, (as opposed to hand driven) resulting in compressive stresses that were not relieved, as the cooling of the rivets drew the plate tight against the framing. Rivets are always "driven" red hot. When sulphide particles in the steel are subjected to stress, micro-cracks can become macro-cracks providing ready pathways for fracture crack propagation. A better method of riveting would have been to ream the holes, in effect drill them, which prevents the creation of micro cracks. However this is more expensive and usually only done for warships. What process was generally used on the Great Lakes isn't known but given a shipyard's propensity for efficiency and economy, they were likely punched.

While I can't state this for a fact, it was likely the same "grade" of steel in common use on the Great Lakes. Based on the knowledge of the times, it was not "inferior" steel in any regard. Remember the *Western Reserve* was built in 1890 and the *Gilcher* a year later. The quality and quality control of the steel (from plate to plate) would have been similar. Realize too, the same problem continued through the construction of the World War II Liberty ships. The *Carl D. Bradley*, built in 1927 and *Daniel J. Morrell*, built 1906, would have fallen in the middle of this period of "problem" steel making both (and certainly many others) prone to cracking. It would be very interesting to recover sufficient samples from the *Bradley* and *Morrell* which are located and the *Gilcher* and *Western Reserve* when finally found, to see what role brittle steel played in their loss.

LOST OFF THE KEWEENAW - THE *HUDSON*

The gale that sank the *Hudson* was a powerful one blowing hard for several days. Smashing into Keweenaw Point with unusual ferocity, it knocked down electric power and telephone lines, isolating the lonely Appalachian-like area even more than normal. Shipping was hard hit, with many steamers sheltering in Portage Lake until the weather calmed. And out on the wild lake a steamer was in desperate trouble.

Again and again the rolling southwest seas slammed into the steamer's stern quarter, each sending a deluge of water high over her storm ravaged wheelhouse. Pushed on by the straining engine, her steel bow continued to cut through the gale-wracked lake. Far behind was the sheltered water of Duluth harbor where she loaded a cargo of 69,000 bushels of wheat and 22,500 bushels of flax. Far ahead was Buffalo where she would discharge the grain, earning a good freight. As common in the days before safe load limits were strictly observed, the dockside agents loaded her with as much grain as they thought prudent and likely a bit more for good measure.

The southwester slowly built in power and the heavily loaded steamer's deck was swept by the tumbling waves. Tons of water cascaded over the steamer with each sea, much of it running into the cargo hold through damaged hatches and more flowing below decks via smashed cabin fittings. Her pumps worked overtime trying to expel the torrent of water.

As the powerful assault continued the steamer began to roll to sickening angles, each time reaching a point further over than before but each time coming back. Finally the cargo could defy the laws of physics no longer and the grain shifted with a deep rumble heard above the roar of the storm. In desperation the captain tried to heave to and somehow ride out the gale but

Went Missing Redux

she soon went over on her beam ends. A distress flag whipped vainly from her tilting mast.

A ship goes on her beam ends when listed to an angle where her beams (underdeck beams) are almost perpendicular to the sea and her righting power gone so she doesn't return to an upright position. This condition usually occurs when the cargo shifts or in some instances, especially in sailing ships, being hit by a sudden and powerful squall or sea inducing too deep rolling. Going on beam ends is a virtual death sentence.

Hours later another steamer loomed out of the gray edge of the roaring gale. To the crew on the *Hudson* she represented heaven sent salvation. Surely she would stop and somehow rescue them from certain death. Looking closer the crew realized the stranger was in desperate trouble herself. She had her own struggle for survival and couldn't help anyone.

At times the new ship looked to be completely engulfed by the waves, emerging each time with great torrents of water pouring from her deck. But unlike the dying *Hudson* she was winning her fight. Clearly though, she had no capability to assist them. Whether the *Hudson* lived or died was beyond outside help. With their hopes smashed, the crewmen one by one resigned themselves to their ugly fate.

The *Hudson's* starboard rail was already two feet underwater and her long steel keel exposed to the gray daylight. Each wave running over her threw more and more water into her holds. Forlornly the crew watched as the stranger slowly disappeared back into the gale, an apparition of hope turned to hopelessness.

It wasn't long after that the *Hudson* dove for the bottom of Superior quickly ending the lives of her 24-man crew, most hailing from the Buffalo area.

It was Monday September 16, 1901 and within acceptable limits of conjecture, these were the circumstances surrounding the loss of the Western Transit Line steamer *Hudson*. The Western Transit Line was the lake fleet of the New York Central Railroad. Now for the hard facts surrounding the disaster.

At first marine men thought the *Hudson* died a lonely death, unobserved by anyone. However there was one witness to at least part of her demise. During the later official investigation a Miss Bennett, the daughter of Eagle River Lighthouse keeper Thomas Bennett told the Western Transit Line agent she watched an unknown steamer clear Eagle River about 8 a.m. on September 16. She remembered the lake was blowing a whole gale and the steamer was having a very difficult time. She watched the ship's lonely battle through her father's marine glass for two hours before the steamer disappeared about two miles offshore. Either she just faded into the gale or foundered. She couldn't tell.[i]

Lost Off The Keweenaw - The Hudson

Eagle River Lighthouse circa 1900. Did the lightkeeper's daughter actually see the Hudson *sink in front of her eyes? Author*

Eagle River is just 25 miles west of Keweenaw Point. The shipping lanes for lake traffic running the south shore route to and from Duluth - Superior are just a few miles offshore so the keeper's daughter was well familiar with not only vessels but also the area's infamous storms. She was a very experienced observer.

It wasn't confirmed until the 20th the lost vessel was the *Hudson* when a yellow and black spar, the steamer's colors, was found ashore north of Eagle River.

The following day the Portage Life-Saving Service Station crew began the tedious job of searching the shore for other wreckage and bodies of the crew. There was no thought any sailors could have survived the sinking. The beach patrol found nothing from the wreck but the steamer *J.C. Ford* did.

The *Ford* was coming around Keweenaw Point 35 miles from the supposed scene of loss when she sighted the *Hudson* wheelhouse floating along in the waves. Looking closer *Ford* sailors were startled to see the steamer's first mate still inside. He was very dead and a life jacket was tied securely to his waist. The *Ford* continued on to Marquette and wired the news back to the Keweenaw searchers.[ii]

In the meantime more wreckage began to appear along the shore of Keweenaw Point. Lightkeeper Henry Corgan at Copper Harbor found a rope

Went Missing Redux

The New York Central steamer Hudson. *Author*

box painted with the name *Hudson*, a bell rope, several sashes and doors, bedding, pillows, mattresses, a yawl boat with all oars securely lashed down and painted with *Hudson* across the stern, several hatch covers and an ice box. The lashed oars on the yawl indicated there was no attempt to use the boat, she just floated free when the *Hudson* dove for the bottom. A half-inch rivet squarely sheared in two was found under part of the wreckage, clear evidence of the power of the gale.[iii]

All the wreckage discovered wasn't from the *Hudson*. For example 25 barrels of flour came ashore near Eagle River and it was assumed it came from the wreck. However the Western Transit Line agent who came up from Buffalo to investigate the disaster as well as handle the multitude of associated problems, said no, she carried only grain. Some other ship lost the flour.[iv]

On September 25, a full nine days after the wreck, a fisherman found the bodies of two of the crew washed up on the beach in Little Traverse Bay, on the east side of the Keweenaw. The men were 70-miles from the believed wreck site. Both were still wearing life jackets marked, "steamer *Hudson*."[v]

With the belief the prevailing winds could have blown more bodies into the same area, the steamer *Thomas Friant* searched the coast from Eagle River north past Copper Harbor and east of Keweenaw Point. She would return with the body of the second engineer, George Vought (Voight?) found ashore five miles north of the Portage Upper Entry. The badly decomposed body was naked save for his boots, his clothing ground away by the rocky shore.

Lost Off The Keweenaw - The Hudson

The package freighter Hudson *steaming in calm water. The illustration is by the late maritime historian Fr. Edward J. Dowling, S.J. Author*

The *Friant* nearly wrecked herself during the search. While carefully probing the coast outside Copper Harbor she ran hard up on a sand bar at 10:00 p.m. Had she not been running checked down (very slowly), she would have been severely damaged if not destroyed outright. Luckily a lighthouse tender was in the harbor and hearing her distress whistle, came out and pulled her free.[vi]

As the days passed more and more reports came in about *Hudson* bodies coming ashore. One was found floating just off Manitou Island by lightkeepers George Smith and Arthur Marshall. The keepers hastily (and temporarily) buried it in an old fish box. There was nothing to identify the body other than it's red hair and gold front teeth![vii]

A fisherman at Birch Point, eight miles north of the Keweenaw's Bete Gris, made an especially gristly discovery. When walking along the beach he found a pair of boots sticking up out of the sand. When he pulled at one he was shocked to find a human foot inside. What was thought to be the remains of Captain August McDonald was found in the Tobacco River, ten miles north of Lac La Belle. The remains of both men were quickly buried pending proper disposition.

There was also initial speculation a body found at Pine River near Big Bay in early November was that of Captain McDonald. What makes the body especially interesting was the teeth. When coroner Crary examined the remains he was shocked to discover all the teeth in the upper set were doubled

Captain August McDonald of the Hudson. Author

save three while all the ones in bottom set were single except for doubled back molars. It was a very rare condition and should have made identification easy however Captain McDonald's dentist denied they were his and the body was reportedly never recognized.[viii]

Every possible effort to recover bodies was made. The company even arranged for a small launch to run west from Marquette scouring the coast from Sauks Head, 18 miles west of the city to Pequaming. It took two weeks to probe every nook and cranny of the wild shore but it proved fruitless. It appears virtually all of the remains were sent back to the Buffalo area for interment. But only seven of the 24 men aboard were ever reportedly found. The remainder either made shore and were never found, buried in the sand or hidden in rocky crevices, or still on the cold bottom of Superior.

Note the large openings in the hull for ease of handling cargo. Author

Lost Off The Keweenaw - The Hudson

The captain of the Western Transit Line steamer *Auburn* reported he heard from a source at the Soo a downbound steamer passed through a group of 11 bodies floating near Stannard's Rock Lighthouse. Forty-two miles due north of Marquette and just a few miles south of the main Duluth - Soo shipping lane, it was called the "Loneliest Place in America" by the old lightkeepers due to the remote location. All the floaters were reportedly wearing *Hudson* life jackets. Since the seas were running high the steamer wasn't able to recover any of the dead men, leaving them to finish their drift to nowhere. The *Friant* was sent to investigate but apparently was unable to find them, if they ever existed. By this point searchers were chasing every rumor possible.[ix]

Investigators determined the unknown steamer that passed the *Hudson* in the gale and didn't render aid was the 263-foot wooden steamer *John M. Nicol* of the Union Transit Company. Captain William McLean was severely criticized for his lack of action. Giving aid to a vessel in distress is one of the most sacred traditions of the sea. Failure to do so while not unheard of was considered disgraceful by sailors and public alike. However an official U.S. Steamboat Inspection Service investigation exonerated him from neglect.[x]

The only serious criticism the investigators had was that while Captain McLean was anchored behind Keweenaw Point he failed to report the *Hudson's* plight to the captain of the Western Transit Line steamer *Buffalo* also anchored under the point's shelter. The *Buffalo* was a fleet mate of the *Hudson*. But as there was nothing the *Buffalo* could do about the situation, it wasn't a serious issue.[xi]

Captain McLean of the *Nicol* later stated: "In order to render any assistance it would have been necessary to run to the lee of her and get lines to the crew, as it would have been impossible in that sea to try to save the boat. To run to the lee of the *Hudson* would have meant to sink my own boat and to sacrifice the lives of the 21 persons on board. One roll of the *Hudson* against the *Nicol* would have sent us to the bottom in five minutes. It was a terrible thing to see those men clinging there with not one chance in a thousand of ever getting away and then have to pass them, but it would have been foolhardy to attempt to run close to her."[xii]

He also said he saw a big steel freighter, likely the *Gilchrist*, off to the west and was surprised she did come to the aid of the *Hudson*. Captain Gunderson of the *Gilchrist* later stated he never saw the *Hudson*. The *Gilchrist*, renamed as the *Prindoc*, became a Lake Superior shipwreck victim sinking off Passage Island on June 6, 1941.

After rounding Keweenaw Point, the *Nicol* anchored in the shelter of the east side of the peninsula. She had taken such a severe beating in the gale it took more than 40 hours to pump her out.

WENT MISSING REDUX

The Prindoc, *as the* Gilchrist, *was one of the last ships to see the* Hudson *still afloat. Author*

The *Nicol's* chief engineer took an equally dark view of the gale as his captain, claiming the twisting and wrenching of the ship in the waves was so severe her steam pipes began to work loose. Had the situation become much worse she would have been voluntarily beached to give the crew a fair chance to escape before she sank. Neither captain nor engineer was apparently exaggerating to explain away their lack of help for the *Hudson*. When she reached her final destination she went into drydock for caulking and repairing her arches.

Although there was an apparent witness to the wreck, the lighthouse keeper's daughter, and a number of bodies recovered, the mystery of where the ship actually lay remained. It was potentially solved in early October when Captain Reed of the steamer *Harvard* reported finding a spar protruding from the water off Eagle Harbor. Eagle River was just six miles to the southwest. Reed was running upbound for Duluth in a heavy sea and the spar was only visible in the trough meaning in calm weather it would be below the surface. Regardless Reed noted it's location.

However the agent for the Western Steamship Line discounted the sighting, claiming Reed had a "pipe dream." He said both spars had already been found on Keweenaw Point and that she sank off Eagle River, not Eagle Harbor. In addition the water where Reed saw the "spar" is 600 feet deep, far too deep for a ship's spar to project to the surface. What Reed saw was never identified but it can be postulated it was a log (deadhead) floating end up or it could have been a spar from another vessel just merrily floating along.[xiii]

Lost Off The Keweenaw - The **Hudson**

The exact location of the *Hudson's* sinking remains unknown. The Steamboat Inspection Service placed her between two and eight miles off Eagle River and news accounts generally about two miles, but since there were no witnesses actually seeing her take the plunge, such locations are at best only guesses. Perhaps she even staggered on for a time after the lightkeeper's daughter's observation, only sinking hours and miles later. To this day she remains a mystery, lost somewhere in the cold and dark depths of Lake Superior west of the Keweenaw.[xiv]

Why she sank is much less of a mystery. Remember McLean on the *Nicol* said he saw her on her starboard rail so doubtlessly her cargo shifted. Grain was a cargo notorious for shifting and the steamer carried a full cargo of wheat and flax. Still, without a surviving crewman to tell the tale, this is just an educated guess.

It is also very possible an engine or steering breakdown could have been the problem. Without power or helm command, she would have fallen into the deadly trough of the waves and literally rolled her guts out! If the cargo hadn't shifted earlier, it would have in the trough!

Captain Jones of the 312-foot steamer *Mohawk*, also a Western Transit Company boat, when later interviewed in Portage Lake didn't know what happened to the *Hudson* for certain but suggested she could have hit a rock. Considering the geology of the Keweenaw coast, perhaps it wasn't such a bad idea, especially if she bottomed on Sawtooth Reef.[xv] This infamous ship killer runs about seven miles long and a mile or so offshore, roughly between Ontonagon and Eagle River. The remains of a dozen wrecks pay silent tribute to the danger including half the 580-foot steel freighter *William Moreland* gutting herself on it in 1910. The stern half was recovered but the rest is still there.

Just northeast of the *Moreland* is the 286-foot iron freighter *Tioga*. She destroyed herself on Sawtooth on November 26, 1919 in the midst of screaming gale. All of the crew made shore safely but the ship became a total loss, her cold iron still splayed out on the reef like a peeled banana. She suffered a monstrous tragedy in July 1890 when her cargo exploded while berthed in Chicago; 30 men, mostly stevedores, were killed in the blast.[xvi]

By the standard of the times the *Hudson* was a well-constructed vessel. Built by the Detroit Dry Dock Company of Wyandotte, Michigan in 1888, she was comparatively large, 2,294 tons, 288-feet in length, 41 feet in beam and 23 feet in depth. The *Hudson* was also fast, her 1,300 horsepower triple expansion engine providing turns for 15 mph. A very unusual feature for a package freighter was two smokestacks in tandem.[xvii]

The *Hudson* was a very costly loss to the railroad and underwriters. Including cargo the loss reached $300,000 of which only $211,000 was covered by insurance.

WENT MISSING REDUX

The *Hudson* was the sister ship of the steamer *Harlem* wrecked on Isle Royale on November 26, 1898. The *Harlem* was later recovered but only after a very dramatic salvage. She was upbound for Duluth when she steamed smack into a roaring northwest gale. The blow was powerful but the *Harlem* was well built so the captain kept driving on for port. When the northwest seas eventually grew to 20-feet in height the captain realized things were on the verge of getting out of hand so he swung around to a new course, intending it come in behind Isle Royale and run south in its shelter, then eventually working his way to Duluth. However in flying scud, rain and spray from the crashing seas, the captain couldn't "pick up" the coast of Isle Royale and slammed up the reef just 4-3/4 miles southwest of Menagerie Island. The island is the site of Isle Royale Light, a beacon the captain never saw in the miserable visibility.

The *Harlem* was in bad shape, soon sinking to the point where water reached her spar deck, boilers flooded out and she showed signs of breaking

The steamer Harlem *on launching. She was a sister ship to the* Hudson *and also a victim of shipwreck although salvaged from her Isle Royale perch. Author*

Lost Off The Keweenaw - The Hudson

in two. At the first opportunity the crew launched a lifeboat fleeing to nearby Isle Royale Light for shelter. Whether keeper John Malone was overjoyed receiving his unexpected guests is unknown but certainly he did all he could to make them comfortable. John and his wife raised 12 children at the lonely light, all actually born on the island! Doubtless he and his wife were used to dealing with "crews" and "unexpected arrivals."[xviii]

With prospects for quick salvage nonexistent, the Western Transit Company turned her over to the underwriters who in turn sold her for a song, actually $30,000 which considering the ship was valued at $255,000 was a steal if and it was very big if, the salvagers could actually recover her. The salvage company taking the gamble was a little outfit from Port Huron, Michigan. Most experts didn't give the small guys much of a chance. After all the big outfits all looked at the wreck and didn't think it could be done. Like the little engine that could, the salvagers went to work and the following fall had her off the reef and safe in Port Huron. After subtracting salvage expenses and the cost of rebuilding her to original specifications, they had a substantial profit of $90,000!

Following her salvage the *Harlem* had an unusual career for a lake freighter, having ten owners and ending her days in 1930 as a floating hotel in Jacksonville, Florida.[xix]

The *Harlem* and *Hudson* generally ran in the package freight trade between Chicago and Buffalo, but occasionally were used between Duluth and Buffalo. Normally each boat made 27 round trips a year, with each Duluth - Buffalo run taking just over four days, about the same time a modern freighter would take today.

The Western Transit Line wasted no time replacing the *Hudson*, quickly awarding a contract for a new steamer. Regardless of the contract for a direct replacement, within two weeks of the *Hudson* sinking the new 343-foot steamer *Chicago* was launched, thus becoming the 13th vessel in the fleet. Perhaps there was a bit of the unlucky 13 in her since she wrecked on Michipicoten Island in eastern Lake Superior on October 23, 1929. The actual one for one *Hudson* replacement when she finally came out of the yard was a near twin to the *Chicago*.[xx]

When the *Hudson* dove for the bottom she was under the command of 44-year old Captain Angus J. McDonald. He came from an old sailing family, his father as well as three brothers all being Great Lakes captains. Angus was a veteran of 31 years sailing on the lakes, 23 with the Western Transit Line, 17 of them as captain. He commanded the *Hudson* since the start of the 1894 season. Hailing from St. Catherines, Ontario, he left a wife and four children aged 10 to 19. His total estate was a mere $500 dollars, little enough for a life on the lakes.[xxi]

WENT MISSING REDUX

The captain was no stranger to shipwreck. He was on the wooden steamer *Albany* when she was cut down in a Lake Huron fog off Point aux Barques, Michigan on November 1, 1893 by the steel steamer *Philadelphia*.

The *Albany* stayed afloat for a while because her holds were filled with grain, which swelling from the water, partially plugged the gapping wound in her hull. The *Philadelphia's* bow was stove but her pumps seemed to be keeping up with the water flooding in so she took the *Albany* in tow heading for shallow water. If they could stay afloat long enough both could find an easy sand bottom to slide up on and await repair. It was a short-lived effort. When the *Albany* showed signs of dropping to the bottom, Captain McDonald and his crew fled to the *Philadelphia*. When she also started to settle, both crews took to their yawl boats, 24 men in the first boat and 20 men in the second. Only the second boat survived. Evidently the men in the first were killed when the boat drifted under the still moving propeller of the *Philadelphia* when she dove for the bottom. No blame was attached to McDonald for the loss of the *Albany* and his sailing career continued.

Chief Engineer Moses Trouton was also a member of a shipping family but instead of being deck officers, two of his sons were engineers on lakes boats.

Contemporary news accounts state the U.S. Steamboat Inspection Service held an extensive investigation into the *Hudson's* loss in Detroit on October 5, 1901 however a careful search of the National Archives failed to find a copy of the report. Were there other contributing factors to the loss beyond the gale and shifting cargo, perhaps earlier damage from a collision or grounding? If so could the missing report have shed real light on one of the lake's still undiscovered shipwrecks?

The Hudson *was odd as a Great Lakes freighter in that she had twin in line stacks. Ken Thro Collection*

Lost Off The Keweenaw - The **Hudson**

Eight years later on November 15, 1909 there was an uncannily similar shipwreck to the *Hudson*. The 256-foot Canadian wooden steamer *Ottawa* was downbound from Thunder Bay with grain when a fierce storm overtook her. Her grain cargo shifted when she slipped into the wave trough. In an effort to save his ship the captain placed virtually his entire crew into the holds in a desperate attempt to shovel the grain cargo back into place. In spite of their frantic work to save the ship it wasn't to be and the captain and crew had to leave her in the lifeboat. He pulled his men out of the hold just in time as she rolled and sank shortly after they abandoned her. The *Ottawa* foundered about 15 miles off Passage Island.[xxii] Could Captain McDonald have had many of his men below shoveling when she sank thus accounting for the comparatively few bodies recovered, discounting the supposed sighting of 11 off Stannard's Rock?

The Hudson *battling Superior on her final trip. The pencil sketch is by the late maritime illustrator Edward Pusick. Author*

Went Missing Redux

There is an eerie twist to the *Hudson* story. Considering sailors are very superstitious it is remarkable the steamer was ever named *Hudson*. Sailors always believed a ship should have a lucky name and by judging by shipping records, *Hudson* was anything but lucky. A schooner *Hudson* sank off Conneaut, Ohio in 1859; a steamer *Hudson* perished off Cedar Point, Lake Erie in 1856; another *Hudson* in Lake Michigan in 1894; the sidewheel steamer *Hendrick Hudson* burned in Cleveland in 1860 after being hit with lightning and the *Sarah Hudson* in Lake Erie in 1863 after a collision. The *Hudson* was also claimed to be the 13th ship in the Western Transit Line. A previous number 13, the steamer *Idaho*, sank in Lake Erie in 1897. Naming the new ship *Hudson* was certainly tempting fate![xxiii]

Perhaps the luckiest man on the *Hudson* wasn't. Second Mate Thomas J. Reppenhagen didn't make the last trip. Whether he was ill, quit or had a premonition of disaster isn't known. His place was taken by eager substitute Burt Gray.[xxiv] And so turns the wheel of fate!

Over three years later the *Hudson* made news again. Edward Switzer of Bay Mills in the eastern end of the Whitefish Bay, reputedly discovered a message in a bottle floating near the shore at Iroquois Light. It read, "Capt. of Steamer *Hudson*. Steering engine gave out, we are going. Good by." Local marine men disagreed whether it was authentic or a hoax, just a joke by somebody with too much time on their hands. Three years is a very long time for bottle to bob about the lake. Of course if the steering engine did fail, then the *Hudson* would likely end up in the wave trough and her end was predicable.[xxv]

The *Hudson* has become a bit of a local ghost ship. It seems her dripping rust covered hulk is sometimes sighted drifting silently in a fog-covered lake. Seeing the dead ship is said to be forewarning of a storm.[xxvi]

But the question still remains. Where is the *Hudson*?

A Victim Of Superior Shoal? - The *Bannockburn*

Perhaps more than any other Lake Superior "went missing" ship the disappearance of the steamer *Bannockburn* has inspired tale telling talents of generations of Great Lakes writers. Had she been lost off Florida, the *Bannockburn* certainly would be enshrined with due ceremony as an honored member of the fantasy world of the "Bermuda Triangle." All nonsense aside the loss is very intriguing with elements of real mystery surrounding it. And like many mysteries, there is a possible explanation that is a bit more mundane.

The 1,620-ton steel steamer *Bannockburn* was built in 1893 at Middlesborough, Scotland by Sir Raylton Dix and Company. At 245-feet she had beam of 40-feet and a depth of 18.4 feet. By all accounts she was a well-built and seaworthy vessel. When launched, Lloyd's of London concurred in this endorsement, giving her a rating of A-1. She was owned by the Montreal Transportation Company of Quebec. Ship and cargo were valued at $200,000. Her captain was George R. Woods of Port Dalhousie, Ontario. Located on the Lake Ontario entrance to the Welland Canal, it was the breeding ground for generations of Canadian Great Lakes captains and sailors.

Her last trip started on a bad note. After loading 85,000 bushels of wheat at the Canadian Northern elevator in Port Arthur, Ontario on November 20, 1902 she ran aground while attempting to leave the harbor. It took a while to work free and she didn't depart Port Arthur until the following day. The cargo was intended for Midland, Ontario on Georgian Bay. It was widely thought it was the last trip of the season for her. Little did marine men realize it was her last trip period!

WENT MISSING REDUX

The Bannockburn, *circa 1900.* Author

The *Bannockburn* was seen on the evening of the 21st by Captain James McMaugh of the upbound steamer *Algonquin*. His sighting placed her, "about 50 miles southeast of Passage Island, northeast of Keweenaw Point."[1]

At the time the *Bannockburn* was bucking head into a strong headwind but to those aboard the *Algonquin* she appeared to be running well. The weather was a bit hazy though and she quickly faded from view.

Later in the night one of the worst storms of the season slashed across the central lake.

When the *Bannockburn* failed to reach the Soo on schedule no initial alarm was felt. She was simply posted as overdue. Doubtless the foul weather delayed her. But as the days passed and neither ship nor information as to her whereabouts arrived, the first alarms of concern rang in the maritime community. Perhaps she was sheltering in some lonely port on the north shore or suffered machinery damage and unable to proceed, left to drift on the open lake. Certainly she would turn up all right!

When no word was heard from her by November 27th the owners gave her up for lost. None of the hoped for explanations panned out. The *Bannockburn* was just gone, disappeared, vanished, sailed off into a crack in the lake as the old timer sailormen used to say.

A Victim Of Superior Shoal? - Bannockburn

The following day though an electrifying message reached the Soo and Kingston, Ontario where most of the crew hailed from. The steamer was ashore on the mainland north of Michipicoten Island! Family and friends were overjoyed with the good news. The happy dispatch came from Chicago where the Canadian steamer *Germanic* just arrived and reported supposedly seeing the *Bannockburn* safely on the beach. The tugs *Boynton*, *Ossifrage* and *Favorite* steamed quickly for the area to search for the ship. They combed the area far and wide but never found a trace of ship or crew. Both were nowhere to be found. The tug men could only conclude the *Bannockburn* foundered in deep water and had taken every man aboard down with her. The *Germanic* crew must have been mistaken or perhaps misunderstood by the men on the dock.[ii]

About this time the steamer *John D. Rockefeller* reported steaming through a field of wreckage off Stannard's Rock in mid lake on the 25th. Since the *Rockefeller* wasn't aware at the time the *Bannockburn* had vanished she paid scant attention to the flotsam, not even bothering to look for a name.

The missing steamer dropped from the news until December 12 when Surfman Dean of the Grand Marais Life-Saving Station found a cork life jacket marked *Bannockburn* while on beach patrol. The jacket strings were tied, suggesting it had slipped off a body. Crotch or seat ties to hold people in the preservers were not yet in use. Once the user lost the ability to keep himself in the jacket, he usually slipped out, slowly spiraling to the bottom of the lake. Inspired by the find, the life-savers searched the beach more carefully as well as offshore waters. Nothing more was found.

The Northern Navigation Company steamer Germanic *incorrectly reported the* Bannockburn *safe when she arrived at Chicago. Author*

The lifejacket as a clue to the disaster was relatively unimportant. It could have been lost overboard anytime during the storm with a crewman in it or not. It wasn't uncommon for a sailor to be swept overboard. Finding it at Grand Marais is logical too, given the lake's common northwesterly storms.

The bigger question is why the *Bannockburn* was lost at all? To this day it remains a mystery. One explanation comes from Captain McMaugh of the *Algonquin* advancing the theory the *Bannockburn* suffered an explosion just after he sighted her on that hazy morning of November 21. The explosion would explain why she "disappeared" so quickly from his view and why none of the crew (except perhaps the Grand Marais lifejacket wearer) had time to put on a lifejacket.

However no one on the *Algonquin* heard the noise of an explosion or saw any evidence of one. Remember too, the *Bannockburn* was nearly a new ship, built only nine years before, so a boiler explosion would be very unusual.

Mitigating against the *Algonquin* sighting being the last time anyone ever saw the *Bannockburn* is the tale of the wheelhouse crew of the Northern Navigation Company steamer *Huronic*. She was upbound and battling her way through the storm on the night of the 21st, when she passed what the wheelhouse watch thought were the lights of the downbound *Bannockburn*.

Did the Huronic *sight the* Bannockburn *that last storm tossed night? Author*

A Victim Of Superior Shoal? - **Bannockburn**

Only the lights were visible and certainly one ship's lights look just like any other ships lights assuming they are the same kind of vessel seen from the same angle, so the men couldn't be absolutely certain the unknown ship was the *Bannockburn*. But the *Bannockburn* should have been in the area and the men were certain the lights (especially deck lights as opposed to standard navigation) were the lost steamer. Assuming the *Huronic* sighting is correct, the McMaugh explosion theory isn't possible, at least as advanced by the good captain.

The light at Caribou Island on the Canadian side of the lake also enters into the mystery. The island is 45 miles north of Grand Marais, Michigan and approximately 10 miles north of the downbound shipping lane. It was a major beacon for lake commerce and had the *Bannockburn* made it that far east, her crew would have been looking for it's welcoming beam. However for undetermined reasons the Canadian government shut down the light on November 15, before the official close of the lake navigation and six days before the *Bannockburn* left Port Arthur. The crew of the steamer may not have been aware the light was already dark creating a very dangerous situation. Even if they knew the light was dark, it was a dangerous situation. After all there was a reason the light was on the island to begin with! In the days long before radar and GPS, the island and its offshore reefs were a significant hazard.

The 1955 *Great Lakes Pilot* describes Caribou Island as "about 4 miles long north and south with a maximum width of 1-1/2 miles narrowing to a point at either extremity. The east shore should not be approached nearer than 3/8 mile. Reefs extend northerly and westerly from the north and west shores respectively and a rocky with depths of less than 17 feet extends from the southwesterly side to a point 1 mile SSW, from Caribou Island Light."[iii]

Investigators pondered over the Caribou Light problem. There was fear the steamer might have struck the island and foundered in the deep offshore water. Without the light the *Bannockburn* could have smashed into the deadly rock cliffs or gutted herself on a reef or shoal. Could a crewman or several have reached the lonely island only to die of cold and starvation during the frigid winter? Considering the dark and storm lashed night, the possibility couldn't be discounted. However no wreckage was ever reported around the island so in view of the flotsam around Stannard's Rock, Caribou Island must be discounted as a likely site.

There are clearly three key elements to the *Bannockburn* mystery:
    1. the storm
    2. the lack of bodies in lifejackets
    3. the grounding in Port Arthur.

Certainly the lake was lashed by a powerful storm on the night on November 21. Several captains said it was the worst in years. But yet their ships survived it without apparent undue effort. For example both the *Algonquin* and *Huronic* came through unscathed. Built in 1888, the *Algonquin* was a 245-foot Scots built vessel similar to the *Bannockburn*. Sold to U.S. interests in 1916, she would eventually go saltwater and become the first American ship sunk in World War I when torpedoed off the Scilly Isles, England in 1917. The 321-foot *Huronic*, a passenger and freight steamer, was built in 1902. The *Bannockburn* shouldn't have had any particular trouble in the gale either.[iv]

The *Bannockburn* at only nine years old was a comparatively new vessel and Captain George Woods an experienced master. Her route was one she ran many times before. There was nothing new for ship or crew. It all should have gone like clockwork. The storm alone should not have been her undoing.

Since only a minimum amount of wreckage was found, none of the bodies of the crew and only one lifejacket, it can be surmised the steamer went down very quickly, too quickly for her crew to make any preparations to abandon her.

The Bannockburn *moored in an unknown location. K.E. Thro Collection*

A Victim Of Superior Shoal? - **Bannockburn**

The key to the mystery could be the grounding in Port Arthur on November 20. Since the *Bannockburn* was fully loaded with grain ready access to her cargo holds to check for internal damage was impossible. She would have to be completely unloaded for a full examination of her holds. Apparently no effort was made to put a diver down to check the bottom plating either. Going aground wasn't new to the *Bannockburn*. Thirteen months prior she stranded at Sand Beach on Lake Huron requiring the effort of the local Life-Saving Service crew to free her. It is entirely possible the steamer suffered more extensive damage than realized at Port Arthur, perhaps even compounding the Sand Beach damage.[v]

The severity of the damage may have only revealed itself in the midst of the storm when the bottom (hull plates) suddenly fell out of the ship. It would have been catastrophic, ship and crew on a quick one-way trip to Davy Jone's locker. In more clinical terms it is reasonable to assume she foundered due to storm stress compounded by the hull damage.

A similar end befell the steamer *Onoko*, the first iron bulk freighter on the Great Lakes. She was upbound from Collingwood to Duluth in 1915 when she sank off Knife Island, Lake Superior. Built in 1882, it was conjectured she damaged her bottom earlier and started dropping hull plates as a result. All of the 18-man crew escaped. Could the *Bannockburn* have suffered a similar fate?

The *Bannockburn* mystery deepens with the supposed discovery of an oar on the Michigan shore by an old trapper 18 months after the wreck. It was reputedly buried deep beneath a pile of driftwood. Part of the oar was wrapped in an old tarpaulin. When he pulled the oar out of the tarp the trapper noticed the letters B-A-N-N-O-C-K-B-U-R-N carved deeply into the wood. Here the tale gets a bit macabre. To make certain the lettering would stand out, each cut was said to be filled with dried human blood! The tarpaulin was there to protect the lettering. While it is certainly a great story it's likely more fantasy than fact.

There is also the Superior Shoal theory. Superior of course is the biggest and deepest of the Great Lakes. When sailing well off shore, in what could be called the middle of the lake, the last problem a captain would expect to encounter is shoal water. Prior to August 1929 it was thought all the dangerous and uncharted reefs had been discovered. It wasn't like the old days when Captain Charles Stannard stumbled across the reef in 1835 that came to be called Stannard's Rock. Located 42 miles nearly due north from Marquette, Michigan it shoots up from the stygian depths to just above the surface like the point of pencil standing on its eraser. Just off the Whitefish Point - Duluth shipping channel it represents a significant danger to shipping, especially in fog or storm. A day mark was built on the reef in 1868 but a full lighthouse

WENT MISSING REDUX

The Bannockburn *under full steam by the late maritime illustrator Edward Pusick. Author*

wasn't completed until 1882. It proved to be the most expensive and difficult light constructed on the Great Lakes, and the most remote from land. The old keepers called it the, "loneliest place in America" and they were right.

But Stannard's Rock was found nearly a century before. Surely there weren't any more hidden reefs lurking out there, or were there?

In was a warm and calm day in August 1929 as the U.S. Lake Survey vessel *Margaret* was taking routine soundings across Lake Superior. The Canadian Hydrographic Survey had charted their side of the lake out to the 100-fathom line and the U.S. finished the southern part to the international border but a large gap remained in the middle. The *Margaret* was working to fill in the blank spaces as assistance to the Canadians. Everyone considered it all deep water so there wasn't any special urgency about getting the job done. Captain William Green commanded the *Margaret* and Harry F. Johnson ran the survey operation. Both were men with long experience.

It was an age before the Global Positioning System satellite array (GPS) or even the Long Range Navigation system (LORAN) so to mark their course the crew set a series of "brush" buoys at three mile intervals on a line from

A Victim Of Superior Shoal? - **Bannockburn**

the tip of the Keweenaw Peninsula to Passage Island just off the north tip of Isle Royale. In turn the sounding lines ran perpendicular to the buoy line on a northeasterly course. The buoys were made from small trees cut on Cove Island, Ontario, thus inexpensive "brush" buoys were created.

During one of the survey runs Robert C. Hanson was operating the electronic depth finder, a new instrument for the Lake Survey. The machine steadily recorded depths of 600 - 900 feet, exactly what was expected in the middle of the lake. Inexplicably the depth finder suddenly jumped to the top of the scale before dropping back into the expected deepwater range. The only person on the boat who noticed the strange reading was Hanson who was closely watching the readings and noting the results on the field-plotting sheet. Hanson immediately yelled to Johnson but he didn't think it was important, just a glitch in the system. He refused to turn back for another look. Hanson persisted with his argument that something was there and eventually Johnson reluctantly told the captain to come about.

Hanson's claims were quickly validated when the fathometer flashed 45-feet before plunging to 400 feet. After dropping a buoy on the high spot they continued the normal survey. Since the shoal was in Canadian waters a detailed investigation wasn't their responsibility. When the *Margaret* reached port the Canadians were duly notified of the remarkable discovery.

The next year the Canadian Hydrographic Service steamer *Bayfield II* completed an extensive charting of the shoal area and the results were shocking! It ran roughly 2-1/2 miles long and a mile wide with the shallowest spot a bare 21-feet deep and 100-feet in diameter. A 30-foot spot was about 3/4 mile to the southward. Obviously the shoal was a great danger to navigation, especially during stormy weather when a ship plunging in a seaway could smash herself to pieces on the unexpected rock bottom! One

The Canadian survey vessel Bayfield II. *Author*

Canadian hydrographer described it as "...virtually a mountain, rising out of the blue depths..." and it was soon named "Superior Shoal."[vi]

The Canadian *Bayfield II* had a colorful life. The original Canadian survey boat was the *Bayfield I*, a 100-ton wooden tug built in the United States in 1863 and purchased by the Canadians for hydrographic work in 1884. While successful she was too small and too old to do the bulk of the work on Lake Superior so in 1901 the twin screw, 276-ton ocean going tug *Lord Stanley* was purchased. Built in Scotland in 1889 the steam-powered vessel was 140 feet long. She was renamed *Bayfield II* in 1903. When Canada was drawn into the

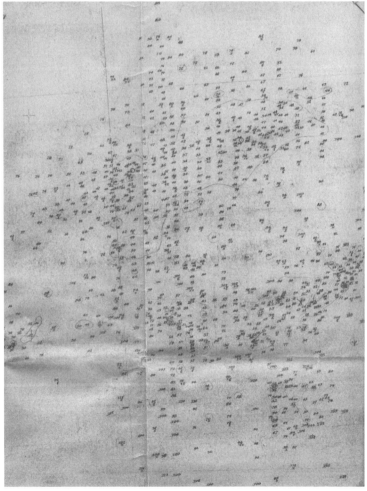

The original **Bayfield** *survey sheet for Superior Shoal showing several points of extreme danger. Author*

A Victim Of Superior Shoal? - **Bannockburn**

ravages of World War I the tug was loaned to the Royal Canadian Navy for patrol duties, returning to survey work in 1919. From 1922 until 1928 she was either under repair or loaned to the Department of National Revenue for east coast duty. (The Canadians weren't quite as warped as America was during Prohibition but they weren't far behind). She returned to survey work in 1929. Decommissioned in 1931 and sold privately in 1937 she sank off Newfoundland in 1949. Both *Bayfields* were named for the famous British nautical surveyor Henry Bayfield.[vii]

Located 38 miles from the Slate Islands on the Canadian side of the lake, the shoal was right on the Passage Island - Michipicoten Island steamer course. The upbound Soo - Passage Island course was only 17 miles to the southwestward and the Soo - Battle Island course 14 miles to the northeast.[viii] The shoal was in the middle of everything!

When the crew of the *Bayfield II* returned to port they told some fantastic tales, ones that really caused folks to think! In one shallow spot the tallow in the sounding lead didn't bring up gravel or sand as expected. To the men on the boat the bottom seemed more like a wreck than a reef. To help determine what was really on the bottom, they pulled a grapple through the area. Instead of bouncing over the rock as it normally would have done, it snagged something that yielded, like the standing rigging of a vessel. They ran the grapple through several more times but the only thing they could pull up was an axe that looked new and undamaged. Obviously it hadn't been tossed overboard by a passing vessel as broken. The crew was convinced they were working over a wrecked steamer lying on the slope of the shoal. The *Bayfield II* was outfitted with a non-recording echo sounder in 1929 but it proved to be inaccurate in shallow water so the surveyors were forced to use the old sounding lead. If the echo sounder was working, would it have picked up the potential wrecks?

A hazard as dangerous as Superior Shoal needed to be marked but nothing worked. The Canadians tried to anchor spar buoys on it in 1934 and later whistle, bell and radar reflector buoys but all were driven off station by wind and wave. They gave up trying to keep a buoy on it in 1954. Mariners as well as newspapers advocated a lighthouse but the Canadian government refused to build one, apparently claiming it was too difficult and too expensive. Considering the construction of Stannard's Rock light in Lake Superior and Spectacle Reef on Lake Huron by the U.S. Lighthouse Service, it was clearly possible, but it seems that the government lacked the political will so it became a case of "mariner beware."

While the shoal was unknown by mariners driving the big freighters American and Canadian fishermen were well aware of it. When the *Bayfield*

WENT MISSING REDUX

A lighthouse similar to Stannard's Rock Lighthouse could have been built at Superior Shoal had the Canadian government had the political will to do so. Apparently it was easier to say "sailor beware" than mark the hazard. Mark Yankovich

surveyed it in 1930 it found the fish tug *Columbia* out of Eagle Harbor working it. It was also believed fish tugs from Grand Marais, Michigan, regularly fished the shoal. Nets were also strung over the western part of the reef. Since the *Columbia* was an American boat, it was also poaching in Canadian waters, a violation of Canadian fishing regulations so it was no surprise she didn't hang around to be questioned by the *Bayfield*. Canadian fishermen also worked the shoal and were just as secretive as the Americans. The fishing was remarkably good so why would the fishermen let the secret out?

When the discovery of the shoal was announced many mariners began to put two and two together and coming up with four. Could the *Bannockburn* have blundered into the shoal? Crashing into it during the gale she would have literally torn her bottom out, sinking in mere minutes without the crew having time to even realize what happened. For that matter, what about the *Inkermann* or *Cerisoles*? Could one, two or three of these "went missing"

A Victim Of Superior Shoal? - Bannockburn

ships be lying somewhere on or around the shoal? Did the *Bayfield's* grapple slide across their decks? Underwater exploration of the shoal has been fragmentary so the answer is still out there... somewhere![ix]

But if Superior Shoal wasn't the answer then what was? Judging from the wreckage location near Stannard's Rock, the single recovered lifejacket and the *Huronic* sighting, the ship likely foundered northeast of Stannard's Rock. Beyond that simple conclusion is the obvious problem, it's a very big and deep lake.

The ship was likely named after the Scottish town of Bannockburn, just south of the City of Stirling. The Bannock Burn is a stream running through the town before reaching the River Forth. The Battle of Bannockburn on June 24, 1314 was also a significant Scottish victory in the first War of Scottish Independence.

The *Bannockburn* remains one of the great mysteries of the lakes. Many fanciful tales surround her loss and phantom sightings. According to some writers her ghostly form has been seen gliding spectrally through storm tossed seas, a kind of freshwater "Flying Dutchman." Supposedly such sightings are most common during the late fall when snow falls thick and fast and a lookout catches only the briefest glimpse of the ice covered *Bannockburn* as she steams on into another world.

One fact about the *Bannockburn* is clear. She still is missing.

"Freshwater, Bah!" - The *Adella Shores*

During the turn of the 20th Century the bulk of the cargoes moving down Lake Superior consisted of iron ore, grain and lumber. "Normal" bulk freighters could easily handle the ore and grain but it took a specialized vessel to efficiently haul the huge amount of timber moving down lake. Over time these special craft acquired the moniker "lumber hookers." Built of wood, they were smaller than the big steel freighters and able to load from minor harbors and in some cases even off the beach, the timber being rafted out and loaded by onboard sheers or ramps. Wherever the lumber was located the hookers would try to work their way in to pick up cargo. The hookers had relatively high fore and aft cabins, which helped protect the stacks of lumber piled on their open decks. Often they towed long "strings" of schooner-barges stacked high with lumber.[i]

The great forests of the lower lakes were depleted of timber much sooner than those in the Superior country. The great cities of the south, Chicago, Milwaukee and Detroit for example had an insatiable appetite for building material. With the lower lake's forests gone, lumberjacks and sawmills moved north and trees from Lake Superior forests soon felt the cold bite of axe and saw and the lumber hookers began their long sail south to market.

Upbound hookers often carried coal or whatever cargo could make a profit. Downbound of course it was always lumber. One such hooker was the *Adella Shores*.

One of the great maritime traditions whether on saltwater and fresh is christening a ship by breaking a bottle of alcoholic beverage across her prow. The symbolism of the act dates back thousands of years.

WENT MISSING REDUX

For example, when the Egyptians, Greeks, and Romans launched a new ship they regularly called on their traditional gods to protect the vessel. The gods Poseidon and Neptune were invariably honored by a toast of wine in recognition of the sacred event.

Jews and Christians also used wine when invoking God to safeguard their ships. Often a swarm of various saints was involved too! Since St. Vincent of Saragossa was the patron saint of wine merchants, doubtless he was the leader of the holy host.

The Ottomans prayed to Allah, sacrificed sheep and feasted (alcohol is a religious taboo). The Vikings took the ceremony to a new level, reportedly even sacrificing a virgin female slave or two as well as quaffing buckets of good mead to ask favor from the gods. Of course they were venturing forth on the cold northern seas instead of benign Mediterranean so a little extra sacrifice was certainly in order.

Things changed a bit during the Protestant Reformation. If a British sovereign was officiating he threw wine from a great cup over the ships foredeck but only after taking a draught (or two). For a while the cups were tossed overboard as a further offering but as the number of launchings increased and the price of cups rose, this practice stopped. Eventually the tradition of breaking a bottle across the ship's bow replaced throwing the libation.

The effeminate French took a little different approach presenting a bouquet of flowers while a priest blessed the boat with holy water. In many ways this explains the usual lack of French Naval success when pitted against a "real" navy.

During the Revolutionary War in America copious amounts of rum based punch were consumed by workmen, guests and passersby in honor of the launch. When the frigate *Constitution*, the greatest navy vessel ever built, was launched, her captain smashed a bottle of good Madeira wine across her stem. Perhaps he did it as a way of recognizing the old British practice; after all, the young American Navy drew its traditions from the Royal Navy.

No matter who christened an American ship, man, woman, merchant or cheap politician, it was always a bottle of booze smashed across her bow with the exception of seawater once in a while. Even during the depths of the American insanity called Prohibition, enterprising shipyards managed to come up with the necessary "bottle" to break across the stem. Evangelical zealots be damned, the gods needed to be appeased! The newspapers may have said the bottles were filled with something else but most folks knew what they really contained and of course the newspaper reporters all had a snort or two of the good stuff to steady their pens![ii]

"Freshwater, Bah!" - *The* **Adella Shores**

The tradition of smashing a bottle across the bow is still followed today. Marinette Marine Corporation in Marinette, Wisconsin, recently finished building 14 -175-foot Keeper class buoy tenders and 16 - 225-foot Juniper Class buoy tenders plus the multi purpose boat *Mackinaw II*.[iii] All were for the U.S. Coast Guard. In every instance the company made certain that the launching ceremony went off without a hitch, that when the sponsor broke the bottle of champagne across the bow of each boat everything went as smooth as could be. Not only did the company rehearse the "swinger" they also deeply scored the bottle to assure it would break easily. There is no reason to take unnecessary chances.

As stated, with rare exception the bottle has always contained an alcoholic libation. The *Adella Shores* was one of those exceptions. Since Miss Bessie Shores, daughter of the owner and sister of the namesake, was apparently an adherent to the Women's Christian Temperance Union, the bottle was filled with freshwater. The new boat was named for her sister Adella. Local old timers must have looked on in dismay, shaking their heads with resignation when they realized the sacrilege occurring. "Didn't those damn fools know it was bad luck to christen a boat with bah, water?"[iv]

The 195-foot, 734-ton *Adella Shores* was built by the Wolverine Shipbuilding Company in Gibraltar, Michigan in 1894 for the Shores Lumber Company. After the hull was launched in Gibraltar she was towed to Ashland, Wisconsin where the company's mills were located for a formal launching in Chequamegon Bay.

The still unfinished steamer but at least now christened, was towed back to Gibraltar for finishing touches. Bringing the hull all the way up to Ashland and then back to Gibraltar was a very expensive gesture.

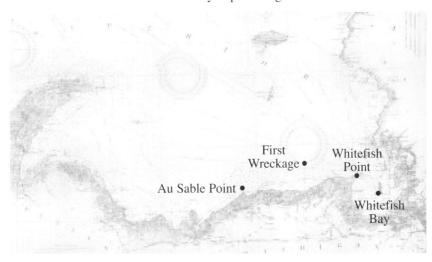

Miss Adella Shores crossed path with her namesake when she married another lumberman, a Mr. Walker from Duluth. It was arranged she and her new husband would take the steamer to Mackinac Island for their honeymoon. As the happy couple approached the harbor (Ashland) following the ceremony she was awed by a most extraordinary sight; an extensive string of bright electric lights running from shore, down the dock and to the boat, up one mast and down the other! Her brother had deftly arranged the surprise for her and his new brother in law! She later said, "It was the prettiest thing I ever saw." Every mill and boat in the harbor also saluted the couple with their steam whistles too![v]

The Adella Shores *was a handsome ship and typical of a lumber hooker. Note the wheelsman in the open pilothouse.* Author

The *Adella Shores* was considered one of the best looking boats in the lumber trade and when launched, was among the biggest of the hookers. Her captains also considered her a very handy boat and would moor to her Ashland dock without using tugs. This certainly contributed to her overall profitability. Her single steam engine developed a reasonable 775 horsepower sufficient to tow her frequent consorts *Constitution* and *Middlesex*. The trio became a familiar sight on Lake Superior.

In spite of the family connection, in 1898 the Shores Lumber Company sold her to the Neff Lumber Company interests. A decade later Neff sold her

"Freshwater, Bah!" - *The* Adella Shores

The Adella Shores *locking through the Soo. K.E. Thro Collection*

to the Manx Transportation Company of Cleveland fro $30,000. Throughout this time she continued in the lumber trade although with a number of scrapes and sinkings. In 1901 she sank in Duluth harbor after striking a deadhead punching a hole in the bow. Luckily the captain was able to make it to shallow water before she settled. After a quick patch job she was back in service.

A similar accident happened in December 1898 when the steamer was working her way through thick harbor ice at Manistee, Michigan. After a tough struggle with the floes she arrived at her dock only to sink to the shallow bottom as the result of several stove bow planks. Raising her and repair was quick and comparatively inexpensive.

The following year she collided with the tug *Ella G. Stone* in the Duluth-Superior harbor, sustaining relatively minor damage.[vi]

In late December 1901 she sank in 18-feet of water at the dock of a West Superior sawmill after striking a piece of heavy ice. She was shifting from one dock to another when the accident happened. Although she settled very quickly, all of the crew escaped easily except the engineer, the water pouring into the engineroom so quickly he had a near thing rushing up from below with the cold lake nipping at his heels![vii]

The first worry concerning the *Adella Shores* reached the Soo on May 7, 1909 when a downbound steamer reported passing through a large wreckage field between Au Sable Point and Whitefish Point. Since it is a distance of approximately 50 miles between the two locations, the report wasn't much value in placing the wreck. The sailors said they saw a pilothouse, cabin furniture, a yawl boat and skylight floating in the waves. Obviously disaster overtook some boat but which one?

When he heard the report the captain of the big steel freighter *Glenellah* remembered an earlier incident. He revealed when hauling his anchor off Whitefish Point on the afternoon of May 3 he brought up a mast and rigging from a wooden steamer. To the captain the ropes appeared not to have been underwater very long. Could he have inadvertently found the steamer? Ominously the *Adella Shores* was overdue at Duluth.

The *Adella Shores* passed up the Soo at 8:00 a.m. on Thursday, April 29, 1909 bound for Duluth from Ludington, Michigan. Aboard was 9,200 barrels of salt, a hefty cargo for the old hooker. Not only were the holds filled but barrels were also stacked on deck too! That night the mournful blasts of distress whistles were reportedly heard at Whitefish Point and further into the bay. However the lightkeeper at the point claimed to have heard or saw nothing unusual.

The Adella Shores *loading cargo from a string of railroad boxcars. Note her boom in use. K.E. Thro Collection*

"Freshwater, Bah!" - The **Adella Shores**

Captain Millen of the big steel freighter *Daniel J. Morrell* who passed up with the *Shores* said, "I saw her while we were in Whitefish Bay Thursday afternoon. She crept along behind several of us, following in our wake through the ice. We cleared Whitefish Point about 7:00 p.m. and I judge the *Shores* was at that time about two miles in the rear. A fierce northeast gale was blowing and getting constantly stronger. In my opinion the *Shores* got a few miles out and found things too rough. She was possibly struck by a big cake of ice starting a leak. Captain Holmes then doubtlessly put about and headed for under the Point. With that gale blowing a bad sea was running over there. He doubtlessly got in the trough and with a leak filling her up she simply went out from under them. The wreckage the *Glenellah* pulled up was from a boat that had not been underwater long."[viii]

Far out in the lake the steamer *Simon Langell* discovered more wreckage. Mate Spaulding reporting, "It was about 6:00 a.m. Tuesday (author's note: May 4) that I noticed that we were passing some wreckage. Suddenly Captain Geel pointed off to starboard. Look at that. I looked and saw the upper works of a vessel about 1,000 feet from us. There was no name seen but the captain who knew her well, said it was the *Shores*. I knew the *Shores* also and agreed with him. We were then about twelve miles northeast off Grand Island. Two days after we arrived at Portage Lake, (author's note: roughly in the middle of the Keweenaw Ship Canal) the steamer *Gettysburg* came in and reported passing part of a pilothouse with the weather canvas on it, parts of a cabin containing a mirror and skylight. No name was visible on any of the flotsam. An hour later the *Gettysburg* saw a yawl boat floating by. We also learned from the *Mills* at Portage Lake that she had sighted a cabin in the same vicinity that we had seen the other wreckage." Finding a wooden cabin or even an entire pilothouse floating as part of a wreckage field wasn't uncommon as both often separated from a sinking ship.[ix]

Shores wreckage continued to be found. The steamer *Northern Light* discovered another field 60 miles east of the Huron Islands and 25 miles north of Grand Island. Although none was marked with the name, it matched the colors and her captain had no doubt it was from the *Shores*.[x]

On May 8, Captain Truedell and his Grand Marais Life-Saving Service crew reportedly found a life preserver marked "*Adella Shores*" and one of the signboards on the beach.[xi] Another report claimed the board was discovered afloat by a Grand Marais fish tug a dozen miles to the west of the village.[xii] Whether found ashore or in the water or meant two boards or confusion over only one was unimportant in helping to locate the location of loss.

An especially gristly discovery was made on May 20 by the Marquette fish tug *Columbia*. While returning to the city from setting nets near Grand Island she ran across unmistakable flotsam from the *Shores* five miles from Grand Portal. Usually such wreckage is just bits and pieces of a ship, without sign humans ever were present. This was very different consisting of a 20-foot square section of her deck with a hole forced through it and an oar marked "*Adella Shores*" projecting through as a makeshift steering rudder. There was also a coat with a union card made out to Peter Olsen of West Allis in the pocket. It can be surmised Olson at least survived the *Shores'* last moments, found the piece of deck and managed to make it into a rough raft with the hope of either sailing to safety or being found by another ship. Perhaps other crewmen were aboard too. Why the jacket was not worn is a mystery. It was spring and ice still clogged the lake. Certainly it was cold enough for a coat. But now the raft was empty, stark testimony to friendless death on icy Superior. What human drama must have played out on that lonely raft.[xiii]

It is interesting to speculate what happened to her cargo of barreled salt. Originally it was thought by marine men the salt would quickly dissolve resulting in hundreds of empty wood barrels bobbing around the lake. But none ever appeared leading the vessel men to conclude either the salt didn't dissolve or the wreck sank relatively intact and the barrels were still trapped in the cargo hold.

The *Shores* could also be called the "Brother Ship" as she carried three sets of brothers. Thirty-seven year old captain Samuel Holmes of Milwaukee, also part owner, had his 25-year old brother Olaf aboard as part of the 14-man crew.[xiv] Fred and George Gabrielson and Peter and Gustav Olsen completed the trio of siblings. All the crew came from only four locations, Milwaukee and Oconto, Wisconsin and Grand Haven and Saugatuck, Michigan.[xv] Some Duluth newspapers stated a crew of 13 were aboard reflective of the typical confusion of number of men aboard in an age of lower personnel accountability. Had she sank in the Bermuda Triangle instead of Lake Superior this ill-omen would have raised her to legendary status.

Even though the Shores Company no longer owned her Mrs. E.A. Shores, the mother of the namesake, who was in Ashland visiting her daughter, told the local reporters she felt the loss of the boat nearly as keenly as if it was still part of the family.

Regardless of what might have been, the *Adella Shores*, christened with water, remains missing on Superior with her crew of 14. Not a single body was ever recovered.

The *Shores* wasn't the only victim of the lake gale. When she was fighting through the ice behind the *Morrell* the 352-foot steel steamer *Aurania* was all but history. Upbound with coal, the ice grabbed her so powerfully she was literally crushed to death off Isle Parisienne in Whitefish Bay in spite of her

"Freshwater, Bah!" - The **Adella Shores**

steel hull! When it was clear she bound for bottom, Captain Pringle and his crew abandoned ship and pushing a small yawl across the ice reached safety at the steamer *J.H. Bartow* three miles distant. Since the ice was rotten in places, the yawl provided a vital safety measure. Several of the men plunged into the icy water but were quickly hauled out.[xvi]

Also upbound from Whitefish Bay on the 29th was the steamer *Schoolcraft* and the 207-foot barge *George Nester* heading for either Duluth or Baraga at the south end of Huron Bay. Depending on the weather, the *Schoolcraft's* captain could put in to either. The pair battled the gale all the way from Whitefish Point and just when it looked like shelter at Baraga was close at hand, the towing hawser broke and the *Nester* was at the mercy of a heartless lake and driving fast for a rock cliff on the north side of East Huron Island. The Hurons are 14 miles west of Big Bay and a bare five miles from Point Abbaye, the turn point for Baraga, the *Schoolcraft's* destination.

The *Schoolcraft's* frantic whistle blasts alerted the Huron Island lightkeeper to the drifting *Nester* but there was little he could do. Powerful waves smashed into the cliff sending showers of spray high into the air. When the *Nester* crashed into the rocks everything was over but the dying, all seven sailors aboard perishing with their ship. None were able to reach the ropes keeper Frank Wittle dropped from the top of the cliffs. Wittle himself was injured when a piece of flying wreckage stuck him, dislocating a shoulder.[xvii]

The Adella Shores *fought a losing battle with the storm. A pastel by the late maritime illustrator Edward Pusick. Author*

WENT MISSING REDUX

What happened to the *Shores*, or more precisely how exactly she sank, is best speculated by Captain Millen of the *Morrell*. He believed she foundered on the night of April 29. Had the captain of the *Glenellah* taken and passed on an accurate bearing of the wreckage he hauled up on his anchor it could have been investigated closer either by dragging or with a hard hat diver proving or disproving it was from the lost *Shores*. Alternatively it could have been from another wreck, not as "fresh" as the *Shores*. The waters off Whitefish Point are littered with shipwrecks so hauling up pieces on an anchor fluke isn't unheard of. Where the wreck of the *Shores* rests on the cold bottom of Superior is open to speculation. None of the evidence points to a definite location.

If only the general locations of the floating wreckage are considered and reflecting on the prevailing wind from the northwest, my guess would place the wreckage about 15 miles northeast of Grand Island. This is generally on the coasting track between Whitefish Point and the Lower Entry of the Keweenaw Ship Canal.

"BUCKING INTO THE TEETH OF THE GALE" - THE *HENRY B. SMITH*

As every Great Lakes sailor knows, the worst time to be on the water is November. When the "gales of November" come calling, smart sailors are snug in a pub, their fingers curled around a glass of "Old Overcoat" or like libation. They aren't out battling storm and gale for one more load of red iron ore. The dead hulls of too many lakers, sail and steam, wood, iron and steel litter Davy Jones's Locker for that!

Everyone is familiar with the *Perfect Storm*, Sebastian Junger's national bestseller about three powerful low pressure areas slamming together off the New England coast in October 1991 causing the loss of the fishing boat *Andrea Gail* with all of her crew. On November 7-11, 1913 the Great Lakes had its own perfect storm and it destroyed far more than a single small boat! When the waters finally calmed, 19 vessels were completely wrecked and 52 damaged. Fifteen of the lost vessels were steamers representing a loss of over $7 million and remember this was 1913 when a dollar had real value. Ten of the ships were lost with all hands! Some the ships are still missing, just swallowed by the Lakes. The loss of life was equally horrific with an estimated 250 sailors killed in what many historians consider the worst storm to ever strike the Lakes.

By any standard, the great storm of 1913 was a hellbender of epic proportions. In terms of pure destruction, no other storm is comparable. The November storms in 1905 and 1940 were each deadly to ships and crews, but only the 1913 storm cut through the Lakes with such fatal force that we still stand in awe ninety-odd years later!

WENT MISSING REDUX

The Smith *making her way up the Cuyahoga River to the steel mills.* Author

The first low swept down from the Aleutian Islands and through the Canadian northwest provinces. A second low rolled in from the Rocky Mountains and collided with the first over Lake Huron. So far this was fairly normal for a fall Great Lakes storm system development, but when a third low roared north from the Caribbean, all hell broke loose. It was a "perfect storm." Forecasters saw the system develop and warnings of the impending tempest were telegraphed to all Great Lakes ports. By Friday morning on November 7, storm-warning flags flew from all the official stations. The freighters generally ignored them; captains thinking, "It's November. Storms are expected and it's our job to drive through."

Storms on the Lakes are just part of normal business. Captains are expected to push on through the normal fall gales without undue delay. The big iron ships made money by delivering cargo on time and not by hiding in port when the gales of November snorted. This was especially true in 1913. The trade had only recently transitioned from wooden ships to iron to steel. A feeling of invulnerability pervaded the industry. With ships as powerful as the monsters coming out of the yards, the captains could bull their way through any gale. This attitude would soon change!

The big iron ore carriers owned by the steel companies made an average of 30 round trips a year between the Lake Superior docks and lower lakes

"Bucking Into The Teeth Of The Gale" - The Henry B. Smith

mills, often returning with coal or light. Smaller freighters owned by independent operators and concerns only averaged 20 round trips.

Only five years before the first of the new 600-footers started rolling out of the shipyards. A single one of these new behemoths could carry a cargo equal to the combined capacity of all of the vessels on Lake Superior at the beginning of the Civil War. In 1895 the average iron ore cargo was 1,800 tons. By 1912 it had jumped to 7,740 tons, all the result of the new bigger freighters. Among marine men the new joke was that the shipyards built them by the mile and just cut them off to whatever length desired.

To make the new big freighters pay they had to be speedy. Fast to load at the docks, fast on the water and fast to unload at the mills. Waiting patiently in port to sail in good weather worked against the need for speed. The 600s were made to bull through the worst the lakes could offer and that's what they were expected to do.

The 1913 storm also devastated land based activities. Traffic was paralyzed, telephone and power lines ripped down by the screaming wind. Snow and ice shut down rail lines marooning thousands of people. Docks

Henry B. Smith *at an unidentified dock. Note the cargo (likely coal) is being unloaded by steam derrick. Archives Canada*

WENT MISSING REDUX

These three photos of 600-foot freighter in a storm clearly show the effects of boarding seas on the open spar or weather deck. The rope (cable) running down the center of the deck is a safely line for crewmen to pass fore and aft. Mentally replace this ship with the Smith *and consider the difficulty she was in with unsecured hatches! Author*

"Bucking Into The Teeth Of The Gale" - The Henry B. Smith

were washed away and factory smokestacks blown over. What happened ashore was only a pale reflection of the devastation afloat. Waves heaped to heights some captains claimed reached 30 feet! Winds screamed at 90 miles an hour! Heavy snow smothered visibility making lookouts useless. In an age before radar the ships were literally running blind, trusting to the gods there was nothing out there in the whirl of white! There wasn't a vessel on the Lakes that wasn't in desperate straits during the 1913 storm.

While all of the Great Lakes were punished by the storm, the worst losses were on Lake Huron. The ships and crews found themselves in the wrong place at the wrong time and paid dearly for the error.

The Interlake freighter *Argus*, in command of Captain Paul Gutch broke in two and sank in Lake Huron with the loss of all hands. Bodies of the crew of 25 washed ashore near Kincardine, Ontario. The wreck was finally discovered in 1972. The *Hydrus*, a sister ship to the *Argus* and another Interlake freighter, also foundered in Lake Huron off Lexington, Michigan, taking her entire crew of 28 with her.

The 550-foot Canadian freighter *James Carruthers*, so new she was only on her third trip, was downbound on Lake Huron with grain from Thunder Bay when storm waves dismembered her. Pitifully few bodies of her crew of 25 were ever recovered.

The five-year-old Hutchinson freighter *John A. McGean*, under the command of 30-year veteran Captain C.R. Ney, was upbound on Lake Huron with coal when she smashed into the storm. The 432-foot steamer was last sighted off Tawas, Michigan before she foundered with all hands. Her broken wreck was finally discovered in 1982.

The small 30-year-old steamer *Wexford* was also in Lake Huron and equally beset by the storm. At some point during the terrible eruption of wind and wave the over stressed vessel was driven to the bottom of the lake. Divers found her sitting upright in 75 feet of water off Goderich, Ontario in August of 2000. The wreck gave no clue to her loss beyond the obvious; an old ship and powerful storm.

While any vessel lost with all hands has an element of mystery, the *Charles S. Price* was particularly inexplicable. She was last sighted in northern Lake Huron near the Canadian package freighter *Regina*. Both ships were fighting for their lives but apparently winning their struggles.

When the storm finally blew itself out and marine men tried to account for their missing ships, they discovered a large freighter floating upside down north of Fort Gratiot Light at the south end of Lake Huron. There were so many ships unaccounted for her identity was unknown. What ship was it? It wasn't until a hardhat diver descended on the dead hull that she was identified as the *Charles S. Price*. Sometime during the height of the storm she had apparently rolled, killing all 28 of her crew.

The *Regina*, a 249-foot Canadian package freighter was also lost and presented a mystery as baffling as the *Price* and intertwined with it. The *Regina* was upbound from Sarnia for the Canadian shore of Lake Superior with a cargo of general freight. She was slowly trying to work her way northward off Harbor Beach, Michigan when last sighted by the steamer *Hawgood*. Her captain remembered, "The seas were breaking over her." It was later surmised that she gave up butting into the waves and tried to turn back to Port Huron and shelter. She didn't make it. Off Port Sanilac, Michigan the *Regina* was crushed by the waves and dove for the bottom. When divers finally discovered the wreck in 1986 they reported her engine room telegraph was set at, "all stop" indicating that the captain had stopped the engines for some reason, perhaps in an effort to allow his crew to make a desperate effort to abandon ship in her lifeboats. In 1913 there was speculation that she and the *Price* may have collided in the midst of the storm causing the loss of both ships. After all, both were seen in close proximity and bodies from the *Regina* and *Price* were also found mixed together on the Canadian shore. The collision theory was fueled by the discovery that some of the *Regina* crew were wearing *Price* lifejackets. The only explanation seemed to be that the *Price* crew hurriedly passed jackets to the *Regina* men in the confusion of the collision. Later the sordid truth was revealed. Apparently local people had robbed the bodies of valuables, including their lifejackets. When they heard the police were coming, the ghouls quickly put the jackets back on the bodies and inadvertently put *Price* jackets on *Regina* crewmen starting the collision rumor.

The freighter *Issac M. Scott*, a sister ship to the *Price*, was upbound on Huron for Milwaukee with coal when the crashing seas pounded the steamer under with the loss of all 28 hands. The wreckage remained undiscovered until 1976 when it was located upside down in 200 feet of water, seven miles northeast of Thunder Bay Island. Previously it was thought she perished closer to the Canadian shore.

The big steamer *Howard M. Hanna Jr.* was bound for Milwaukee with coal on her last trip of the season when the screaming wind drove her aground off Port Austin, Michigan. Battered by crashing waves, the steamer broke in two. An unlikely hero emerged from the wreck when diminutive cook Sadie Black braved freezing waist deep water in the galley to provide food to the trapped crew. Her efforts so impressed the men that when finally rescued by the Life-Saving Service they voted her a special cash purse in recognition of her valiant efforts.

"Bucking Into The Teeth Of The Gale" - The Henry B. Smith

Lightship No. 82 with her entire crew disappeared in the maw of the tremendous 1913 storm. US Coast Guard

Lake Erie suffered its own share of disasters, most notable being the loss of Lightship No. 82. Stationed at the entrance to Buffalo Harbor the sturdy little ship was riding at her mooring when the storm struck but when it finally blew out, the little ship and her six-man crew was gone, wiped off the lake. The wreck was located the following May, nearly a mile to the northeast of its original station. The entire upper works was destroyed, torn to pieces by the battering waves of Lake Erie.

Lake Michigan saw the loss of the big 225-foot schooner barge *Plymouth* off St. Martin Island in the northern lake. The schooner was in tow of the steamer *James H. Martin* when the hawser broke in the heaving seas. Desperately fighting for her own life, the steamer abandoned the *Plymouth* to her fate, condemning her nine-man crew to death.

Ships on Lake Superior faced their own brand of hell. The 227-foot Canadian freighter *Leafield*, owned by the Algoma Central Steamship Line was smashed against Angus Island, fourteen miles southeast of Thunder Bay,

The Leafield *was smashed against Angus Island near Port Arthur – Fort William during the height of the 1913 storm.* Author

Ontario in the western end of the lake. Built in Scotland for ocean trading, she was considered extremely seaworthy. Her entire crew of 18 men perished, swallowed forever by Superior's frigid waters. The *Leafield* could have been considered a doomed ship even before the storm. Both sister ships were lost in the same area earlier. In November 1905 the *Monkshaven* wrecked at Pie Island and the following year the *Theano* sank near Trowbridge Island, both in western Lake Superior.[i]

Another tragedy was unfolding in the eastern lake. The 377-foot steamer *William Nottingham* was slowly working her way into shelter in Whitefish Bay when she went hard up on a reef between Ile Parisienne and Sand Island.[ii] For two days she pounded hard in the grip of the storm. Both her food and fuel ran out. Without the heat from her boilers the men would freeze to death! The fuel problem was partially solved by burning her wood cabin trim and furniture and lastly part of her grain cargo, firemen throwing great shovels of it into the boiler fires. But food was desperately needed. Finally the yawl boat was launched with three volunteers, a wheelsman, oiler and deckhand. With luck they could reach the beach and send for help. The boat barely dropped the falls before it was dashed by the waves against the high steel side of the steamer and overturned drowning all three men. Eventually help did reach the *Nottingham* and the crew was saved. Salvagers later released the ship.[iii]

"Bucking Into The Teeth Of The Gale" - The Henry B. Smith

The 451-foot steamer *L.C. Waldo* was downbound with iron ore from Two Harbors, Minnesota on November 11 when she was plummeted by the booming waves. One rouge wave swept away her pilothouse in a splintering crash of wood. Captain Duddleson, his mate and the wheelsman only saved themselves from being swept overboard by diving down the stairs to the master's cabin in the deck below. Running to the emergency steering station in the stern, her captain tried to bring her around Keweenaw Point using a lifeboat compass illuminated by the flickering light of an oil lantern. He almost made it. Only slightly off course, at 4:00 a.m. on November 11th, she smashed into Gull Island just at the peninsula's tip. Broken in two and with cold dead engines, the ship was an inert beast and her crew knew they would soon join her in the hereafter. They were dead men living. There was no hope for them. If the ship didn't break up under their feet, they would freeze to death! The men of the old Life-Saving Service thought better. Living their motto "Regulations say we have to go out. They say nothing about coming back," two life-saving crews headed into the wild lake, braving 20-foot waves and 60 mile per hour winds. Shortly after dawn on November 11, motor lifeboats from Eagle Harbor, 30 miles distant from the wreck and

Wreckage from the steamer L.C. Waldo *was mixed with wreckage from the* Smith. *Author*

WENT MISSING REDUX

The Henry B. Smith *was known as a "staunch" vessel. Author*

Portage, 80 miles away, reached the *Waldo* wreck simultaneously. The cold was so severe when the life-savers returned to their stations with the *Waldo* crew, they were frozen to the thwarts and family members had to chop them free of the ice! The rescue was so extraordinary both station crews were awarded Gold Life-Saving Medals, only the second such double award in the 44-year history of the USLSS. Ironically the other double award also occurred in 1913. The entire crews of the Point Adams and Cape Disappointment, Washington Life-Saving Stations received the medal for their part in the wreck of the oil tanker *Rosencrans* in January.[iv]

There was no redemption for the *Henry B. Smith* and her 25-man crew however. When she pulled away from the pocket dock in Marquette she and her crew sailed into oblivion.

Built in 1906, the 525-foot, 6,631-ton nearly new steamer was under the management of the Hawgoods of Cleveland. There is some dispute over her name. One source claims it was in honor of a Ludington man who was manager of the Ludington Woodenware Company and owner of the H.B. Smith Machine Company of Smithville, New Jersey. Another source complicates the issue by claiming the H.B. Smith company was actually owned by Hezekiah B. Smith, a New Englander who moved to New Jersey

"Bucking Into The Teeth Of The Gale" - The Henry B. Smith

The Smith *passing under the Duluth Aerial Bridge circa 1910. Author*

with his mistress Emaline. Perhaps half a bubble off level as the old surveyors would say, he was fond of riding around town in a sulky pulled by a moose![v] All considered I like the second explanation best.

    A more mundane but perhaps more accurate explanation is she was named after the vice president of the Smith Steamboat Company of Bay City, Michigan. His wife officially christened her at the launching at the American Shipbuilding Company yard in Lorain. A new feature of the ship was the forward observation tower directly under the captain's bridge. It was designed expressly for guest use.[vi] The Smith Steamship Company was one of 13 concerns owned or managed by Hawgood. Smith's full time responsibility was president of the Michigan Pipe Company but he was also president of the National Bicycle Company.[vii]

At one time Hawgood (technically Hawgood and Avery Transit Company) managed one of the largest fleets on the lakes. The company started in 1881 with schooners and wooden steamers moving into modern steel freighters as technology changed. In 1916 the firm collapsed and was forced into liquidation. It was common during this period for independent vessel owners like Hawgood to organize ships into small, sometimes even one vessel, companies like the Smith Steamship Company. This greatly limited potential liability in the event of a disastrous loss. The collapse followed revelations of stock manipulation and receiving secret commissions (aka kickbacks) from the American Shipbuilding Company for placing orders.[viii]

Valued at $338,000 she was insured for $325,000 and carried $30,000 in iron ore on her last trip. *Beeson's Marine Directory*, the bible of Great Lakes shipping, considered her to be, "One of the staunchest steel vessels on the Lakes." That she would go missing with her entire crew was inexplicable.

Her final trip began at 6:30 p.m. on November 9 when she cleared Marquette's Lower Harbor breakwater downbound for Cleveland with 9,500 tons of ore fresh from the rich Marquette Range. The captain knew it would be a rough trip for the *Smith* and her 25-man crew but the heavy ore would help to stabilize the ship. Superior had been blowing a hard northwest storm but shortly after noon on Sunday it moderated and the captain, apparently thinking the storm was over, left for the Soo Locks.

Many townspeople watched in awe as the big freighter plowed her way out into the still tumultuous lake. One of the most astute observers was Captain Fox of the steamer *Choctaw* in Marquette with coal. Fox would later report he saw the *Smith* "put about" after less than half an hour. Apparently the steamer found the going too tough and headed north for the shelter of Keweenaw Point 60 miles to the west. The rocky Keweenaw Peninsula reaches out into Lake Superior like a long skeletal finger 75 miles long. The closer the *Smith* got to the point, the greater the shelter from the pounding northwesterly seas. She was in effect running for shelter.

Sailors on the steamers *Denmark* and *Choctaw* noticed something else far more ominous. As the *Smith* was clearing Marquette her deckhands were still working to batten the hatches! Since the *Smith* had 32 hatches and each required individual attention, it was a long process. Trying to do it with seas rolling down the decks was virtually impossible.

"Bucking Into The Teeth Of The Gale" - The Henry B. Smith

This series of photos was taken on the Smith *circa 1910. At this writing none of the people are identified. Clearly though, the woman and men in civilian dress are guests to the company. Captain Owen could be the man on the right in the photo of the group in front of the pilothouse.* Author

"Bucking Into The Teeth Of The Gale" - The **Henry B. Smith**

Henry Cleary, the long time keeper of the Marquette Life-Saving Service station also watched the big freighter leave. Seeing her shoulder her way into the big waves he opined surely Captain James Owen would see the folly of continuing on and return to the safety of Marquette. While Owen likely realized the former, he never did the latter. Cleary's station logbook simply stated she was "bucking into the teeth of the gale." It was a classic understatement.[ix]

Soon after the *Smith* departure the lull ended and the storm attacked with renewed fury. The wind, which had been 30 miles per hour when she left quickly rose to 44 miles per hour. The recordings however were taken from a land station. It was blowing far harder on the open lake. Several of the ships that survived the storm claimed wind speeds in excess of 70 miles per hour. The storm continued to howl through Sunday night and into Monday.

Although folks at Marquette expressed fear for the safety of the *Smith* the maritime community as a whole wasn't worried until Thursday, November 13 when she was officially overdue at the Soo. The owners wired every port on the lake inquiring as to the *Smith's* whereabouts but all came back negative. No one had seen the *Smith* after hauling out of Marquette.

Meanwhile, clear proof of an unidentified steamer wreck began to wash up on Marquette beaches. The first wreckage came ashore near the Presque Isle ore dock two miles to the north of the Lower Harbor. Consisting of oak paneling, bits and pieces of furniture and small sections of wood it was definitely from a steamer. But was it from the *Smith*?

Keeper Cleary carefully examined it and thought at least some was from the *Smith* but most likely most came from the wreck of the *L. C. Waldo* breaking apart on Gull Rock Reef at the tip of the Keweenaw.[x]

The news became more ominous when the steamer *Frontenac* docked on Wednesday and the captain reported one of his oilers saw a body floating in a life belt 11 miles east of the city. Rough seas made recovery impossible. Apparently the body never came ashore. Was the floater from the *Smith*?

On Thursday, November 14, landlooker Dan Johnson came into Marquette carrying an oar marked *Henry B. Smith*. He said he found it, as well as three others and part of a pike pole marked *"Henry"* between the Chocolay River and Shot Point. Both are east of the city. The entire area was also littered with small pieces of wreckage, evidently from the upper works of a steamer. Was it from the *Smith* or *Waldo* or both? Past Shot Point the beach was filled with more wreckage including part of a white deckhouse. White was the color of the *Smith's* house.[xi]

Johnson stated the wreckage looked like it had been on the beach for a long time, suggesting it likely came ashore on Monday. The *Frontenac* floater could have been part of the same wreckage field before it reached the beach.

The spar deck of the Smith. *Note the telescoping hatches, one leaf folding over the other in a continuous pattern. The location of the photo is unclear but suggests the lower part of the St. Marys River.* Author

In the days following more reports of wreckage reached the city. William Powell, a fisherman living at Powell's Point near Munising, reported finding flotsam while in his fishing boat below the Pictured Rocks. He brought several pieces back with him including a built in companionway stenciled in red "Henry B. Smith," a marked oar, two cabin doors (white outside and grained inside), two screens for port and starboard running lights, two bed pillows, a green corduroy cushion and an armful of unused life belts. The wreckage was scattered as far as Beaver Lake, 16 miles east of Munising. By appearance, it all came from the *Smith*. Marine men guessed the steamer's superstructure was battered to pieces by the waves, either while actually sinking or before. Additional wreckage was found on the west and north sides of Grand Island.[xii]

Beach patrols east of Marquette continued to find more wreckage, including many wooden hatch covers! Some of the wreckage, including glass fragments from her headlamps, stanchions and a piece of door were brought to the city and displayed in several storefronts. It was after all good advertising! If people came to look at the wreckage, perhaps they could be tempted into the store too![xiii]

"Bucking Into The Teeth Of The Gale" - The Henry B. Smith

The Lake Carriers Association, the trade group of vessel owners and operators, asked local game wardens and deer hunters to keep their eyes open for any bodies if they went anywhere near the beach. So far none were found and it was always important to return remains to loved ones if possible. The search proved fruitless and a rumor that two bodies came ashore near Grand Marais apparently proved groundless.[xiv]

The first remains came into port on the steamer *Saxonia*. She found the body of the second cook Henry Askin, floating in a life belt face down about 50 miles west of Whitefish Point.[xv]

It isn't hard to visualize the *Smith's* last few desperate hours. Shortly after leaving Marquette Captain Owen would have realized the error of leaving a safe harbor for the violence of the open lake. The storm he thought was waning was really rising and he was trapped in it.

The waves were far too high to try to reach the Soo 160 miles distant. All he could do was swing the ponderous steamer to port and try to reach the Keweenaw's shelter. This was the turn the folks in Marquette saw.

Steaming directly into the storm was what heading for the Keweenaw required him to do but there wasn't any real alternative. Mountains of water smashed into her pilothouse then swept down the length of the open spar deck, tearing and grasping at each of the hastily secured hatch covers before battering into the aft cabin. Again and again the same wave sequence happened as the *Smith* fought her way to the northwest. The violence of the storm continued to grow.

Captain Owen fought the great storm with all of his considerable ability gained through 30 years of sailing but he was slowly losing the battle. Once he started to loose hatch covers the fight was over. Great deluges of water were flooding into the cargo holds with every passing wave. Although his big steam pumps clanged away at full capacity they couldn't expel the water quickly enough as it poured through the smashed stern cabin doors and down into the engine room and bilges. Waves ripped doors off their hinges, skylights and portholes smashed in and bulkheads knocked asunder. The lifeboats were long since swept off their davits and blown into the lake. Loosing the lifeboats made no difference anyway. There wasn't a boat made that could survive the terrible tempest or crew capable of launching one in the screaming storm anyway. The end of the *Smith* and her 25-man crew was coming quick.

Ironically though one of the crew did survive. Second Mate John Burk left the ship in Marquette with a severe case of pneumonia. When word of the loss of the *Smith* with her entire crew was telegraphed to his wife, it left no doubt John was dead. Imagine her shock when she received a second telegram not from the company but from her "dead" husband announcing his safety. Very ill and needing his wife's kindly care, he took the train to the Soo where he transferred to another train and another until finally reaching Cleveland and home. Interviewed later he sympathized with his lost crew stating, "It's awful the way men struggle for life when death stares them in the face. God help those poor fellows. I know how it was with the wind and sleet blowing in their faces, beating the breath out of them for hours before the end came. The horror of shipwreck is in the waiting. Pray for sudden and not the grinding, warping, twisting thing called drowning."[xvi]

Burke's wife told the interviewer her thoughts and prayers were with Mrs. Owen. "Its's hard for her, the heartbroken woman, who scans the lake with tear-dimmed eyes." Her comment would fit all the victim's family members. After living with the Adams family, one of the owners of the *Smith*, for a

An unidentified steamer loading iron ore in Duluth. The Marquette pocket docks were identical. Of course the Smith *loading was in the midst of a sleet and snowstorm with frozen ore. Author*

"Bucking Into The Teeth Of The Gale" - The Henry B. Smith

number of years she went to California in 1928 to visit her sister. While there she became ill and died. She wanted to be cremated and her ashes scattered in Lake Superior to be nearer her husband, but as families are wont to do, her sister apparently objected and while she was cremated her ashes were placed in a crypt in Forest Lawn Glendale, far from the icy depths of Lake Superior and her true love.

Born in Ontario in 1858, James Owen took command of the *Smith* when she came out (of the shipyard) in 1906. His previous ship was the 440-foot *Edwin F. Holmes* launched in 1903, which he also brought out of the yard. Clearly he was a captain the owners had great confidence in.[xvii] He was a veteran master with 30 years of experience in sail and steam and considered to be an excellent mariner. He was unusual in that in 1908 he married Mary Ella Cutting, the cook on the *Smith*. Her mother and sisters called her "Pet." At 51 she was a year younger than her husband.

The *Smith* arrived in Marquette late Thursday night, November 6, after being delayed by gales. Friday morning she started to load ore at the South Shore dock but the storm continued to plague her and the loading was far behind schedule. The icey 24-degree weather froze the ore in the dock pockets and had to be knocked loose by hand by dock walloppers using long wooden poles. It was a far longer loading than normal and frustrating to Captain Owen. As soon as the last rock rumbled into the hold, he rapidly headed out into the lake. His deck watch could secure hatches underway. The crews of the *Denmark* and *Choctaw* were witness to the steamer's hurried departure.

Only two of the bodies of the 25 crewmen were ever found. The first was that of the cook found by the *Saxonia* and the second in May of the following year discovered frozen in a block of ice near Goulias Point in the eastern lake by two Indians. Badly decomposed, it was identified only by the papers in his pocket and an inscribed watch as those of the Second Engineer James Gallagher.

A possible explanation for the lack of bodies is that the wind and waves created such havoc along the south shore that the waterline was abruptly changed. Entire stretches of swamp and bayou were filled in with sand making it in time into a solid mass of land. The *Smith's* wreckage was also found higher up the beach, indicating it came ashore at the height of the storm when the waves were at their largest. Bodies driven ashore at the same time could have been buried in the sand, hidden forever.[xviii]

It is also reasonable to assume the *Smith* sank so quickly the majority of the crew had no time to don life belts. The belts should have kept the bodies afloat long enough to reach shore or be recovered by other ships. Accepting this idea, many of the men are still trapped in the wreck.

The steamer Henry B. Smith *downbound to oblivion, a pastel by the late maritime illustrator Edward Pusick.* Author

Speculation why Captain Owen took the *Smith* out into such dangerous conditions ran high amongst marine men and citizens alike. The *Marquette Chronicle* claimed he had been running late all season and was under immense pressure from the owners to, " bring his ship home on time." It was this anxiety to keep his job that forced him to leave when he did.

The Hawgood Company reacted strongly to the *Marquette Chronicle* charge, threatening a civil libel suit against the paper, claiming it was a deliberate falsehood. Whether the action was ever pressed is unknown but every shipmaster is under pressure to make time. Ships don't earn money by sitting at the dock but only by making quick trips with maximum cargo.

Working against the charge of being pressured to "bring his ship home on time" is the fact Owen was an experienced and trusted captain with the company. Not only was he trusted to bring out the *Smith* in 1906 but also the *Holmes* three years prior. Only the most valued captains are given such responsibility. In my opinion the charge is clearly "yellow journalism," an effort to make news, not report it. The quality of journalism in 1913 was no better than it is today.

The question why he left safe harbor when he did has a simple answer. He thought the storm had blown itself out. The worst was passed. He was not aware it was only a lull, a short breather before the storm king blew again. He

"Bucking Into The Teeth Of The Gale" - The Henry B. Smith

knew his run to the Soo would be rough but with a northwest sea on his quarter should be tolerable. Lake Superior in November isn't known as a calm lake. His ship was a staunch and seaworthy boat, certainly able to take a typical November gale in stride.

How much pressure the owners may have placed on Owen is questionable. One marine man stated, "This is of course a delicate question and I would not want to be quoted on it. Naturally the owners want dispatch, but they don't want more dispatch than is consistent with safety. I can't help but believe that the loss of the *Smith* is due primarily to a fatal error in judgment. The storm could not have been underestimated. The Weather Bureaus were still giving the most alarming warnings. The strength and seaworthiness of the *Smith* must therefore have been overestimated. It's a serious thing even to have to think of allotting the blame for such a terrible disaster."[xix]

How and why the *Smith* sank is a more difficult question. Most marine men felt she lost hatches and became waterlogged. While in the act of sinking the thundering waves swept her upper works clean off, accounting for the amount and type of wreckage found east of Marquette. The testimony of the sailors from the *Denmark* and *Choctaw* concerning the unsecured hatches strengthens this explanation.

Mr. J. R. Oldham, a well-known Cleveland marine architect of the era drew a similar conclusion. "The greatest fault with the lake steamers lies in their hatches. The hatch coamings are too low - about 12 inches in height. They should be three feet high. The hatches should be stronger and heavier and more attention paid to the hatch coverings.

"For their size, Great Lakes vessels do not have enough power. With their shallow depth and extreme length they need a great deal of power to make headway against a wind. The average speed possible with the power they have now is nine knots. They should be able to make twelve knots. I don't know that even that would be enough.

"Cargoes of these vessels always should be trimmed. Ore or coal, when loaded into the ships, should be leveled off.

"There is no doubt in my mind but that several of the vessels lost in this storm went on their beam ends in the gale because their cargoes shifted. Shifting of a cargo of ore, coal or grain will send a steamer over on it's side at once.

"Once on beam ends water would pour in through the loosely covered low hatches and the steamer will capsize or sink.

"The reasons why I say lake steamers should have more power is that in those enclosed waters they must be able to keep ahead in a wind. A matter of ten miles out of its course and a steamer goes on the rocks. Unless it is powerful enough to drive on, it is sure to be carried by the wind.

"Lake steamers are of peculiar construction. They are about eighteen times as long as they are deep, whereas the safe ratio of length to depth is twelve or fourteen to one. The type won't be changed because it is the only sort of vessel that can navigate the lakes. The lake steamer must be able to carry a great cargo but it must be shallow.

"So the type and general construction will remain the same. But the remedies I speak of will be made. They are practical and ship owners could adopt the changes if they would."[xx]

As with anyone speaking against the prevailing order of things, Oldham's recommendations were generally scuffed off by vessel owners. But certainly his description of shifting cargo and a ship on her beam-ends, could have accurately described the end of the *Smith*.

The hatches on the *Smith*, as with all steamers of the period, were weak. The covers needed to be covered with tarpaulins for water tightness when foul weather was anticipated. During heavy weather the waves crashing on deck could force the covers off and subsequent waves flood the holds. Although the covers were braced into position, too much reliance was placed on the actual weight of the cover to hold it in place.

There was also speculation the large number of hatches, 32 in total, resulted in a structural weakness in the *Smith's* spar deck. Under the tremendous strain of the gale, the weak deck allowed the steamer to break in two. There is, however, little evidence to support this theory.[xxi]

Another mariner complained about the lifeboats. In a long newspaper interview Mate Gordon Rattray of the Pickands-Mather vessel *H. P. Hope* gave a candid appraisal that echoed testimony from Great Lakes sailors following every major loss to include the *Steinbrenner*, *Bradley*, *Morrell* and *Fitzgerald*. In general terms it is still a problem for "modern" Great Lakes freighters.

"Great Lakes freight vessels carry two lifeboats and raft, sometimes three and a life raft. Each is supposed to carry twenty men. That is the usual size boat. They swing on davits high above the water.

"Not one of these Great Lakes lifeboats is made with ribs. They are made of some sort of plate about one sixteenth of an inch thick, that bends easily - like a galvanized iron pail.

"They are uncovered boats - not decked over in any way. Even if they didn't roll over or fill in a sea, men in them would be exposed to the freezing weather that accompanies the storm that cost so many lives.

"These boats are meant to carry twenty men, are inspected by the U. S. Government inspectors and are supposed to be a means by which men may save their lives in a storm.

"Bucking Into The Teeth Of The Gale" - The Henry B. Smith

"And I defy anyone to take fifteen men in one in a forty mile breeze - that's moderate weather; the Weather Bureau would call it a brisk wind - and get anywhere in it. It would roll over and swamp.

"It would be impossible to lower one of these boats from the davits in a storm. One roll of the ship would smash the lifeboat as a tin pan when it was being lowered. The chances are one in a hundred against ever getting one of them into the water in a heavy gale.

"The loss of lives in the recent disastrous storm is an example of how much these boats amount to. As an experienced sailor I declare that 75 per cent of the lives lost might have been saved had the destroyed ships been equipped with lifeboats which could be lowered or which could be kept afloat and right side up after being lowered.

"Here's an illustration that might give point to my assertion that the lifeboats in use on the Great Lakes now are worse than useless.

"I was at one time second mate of the steamer *Superior City*. At Duluth I saw a U.S. inspector have a boat launched that on her inspection certificate called for twenty men.

"Nineteen men got into her. The captain was ordered by the inspector to make the twenty and the captain refused. The captain told the inspector to get in himself and the inspector wouldn't.

"While they were arguing up above we were down in the boat and I tell you I had to steady that boat at the side of the ship to keep from rolling over.

"There it was, one man shy of the number it was supposed to carry about to roll over alongside the ore docks.

"I wouldn't have dared let it get away from the side of the ship. Finally after neither the captain nor the inspector would get in there being no one else on the ship the boat was ordered back to the deck and that inspector OK'd it.

"There should be a new type of boat on the Great Lakes. There should be a different way of getting it into the water.

"To my mind the ideal boat would be one of steel, 1/8 to 1/4 inch thick, bell or cylinder shaped and decked over with manholes to get into it, and equipped with covers and gaskets.[xxii]

"Such a boat could be launched from a runway aft and shot clear into the water with the men in it - or it could be left on the ship, men could get into it and when the ship turned over or went down, the lifeboat would float off.

"The fault lies with the U.S. government. If the inspectors would refuse to O.K. the useless boats now, there would have to be a change in the model of the lifeboats and in the method of leaving a crippled ship.

"By instructions of the printed rules of our managers and under the U.S. inspection laws, these lifeboats are kept in as perfect condition as possible all through the sailing season.

WENT MISSING REDUX

"I don't blame the lake carriers or ship owners. I blame the government."[xxiii]

A possible reason for the *Smith* loss was uncovered in 1976 when four Wisconsin divers discovered the wreck of the *Issac M. Scott* lost in Lake Huron in the same storm. Located upside down in 175-feet of water, an examination of the wreck showed the *Scott's* rudder ripped loose from the ship. With the rudder so damaged, she would have stood no chance in the storm. Could the rudder on the *Smith* have failed too, perhaps during the severe strain of the port turn to the Keweenaw?

The mystery of why the *Smith* sunk was further confused in June 1914 when a message in a bottle was found by a fisherman at Mamaimse Point on the north shore, 35 miles from Whitefish Point. Dated November 12, the note as printed in the *Marquette Mining Journal* read: "Dear Sir: Steamer *H.B. Smith* broke in two at the number five hatch. We are not able to save her. (line missing) Had one hard time on Superior. Went down 12 miles east of Marquette. Please give this message to owners." The signature was not legible. Torn and faded, the entire message was difficult to read.[xxiv] As typical with such messages, it resolved nothing.

After much debate the *Smith's* owners concluded (at least publicly) the message was a fake. The major reason was the discrepancy in dates. Since it is dated November 12, while the *Smith* left Marquette on the 9th and actually sank late that night or early the next day, the timing was clearly wrong. Did the shipboard writer confuse the dates in the stress of the sinking or was the shore side hoaxer so misinformed to make such an obvious error?

Where the dead hulk of the steamer is located is the big unanswered question. Find her and the chances are the mystery of why will likely be answered at least in part.

The approximate area of foundering could be presumed to be generally north and west of Marquette. This location would match up with the wreckage found on the shore east of the city as blown by a northwest wind. Estimates of the distance from Marquette vary widely, ranging from 40 - 50 miles to as close as 15 to 20. A lack of bodies would tend to indicate the sinking was rapid and most of the crew trapped within. The finding of the cook's body wasn't considered significant since local marine men felt cooks were usually the first in a crew to don lifejackets. They suggested the cook recovered in his life jacket as well as the engineer later found on Michipicoten Island were simply swept overboard during the height of the storm.

Some local marine men however thought the *Smith* was more likely closer to Grand Island. If the bottled message was authentic and the *Smith* sank 12 miles east of Marquette, the resulting wreckage field would have probably washed ashore further east than where it was found working against the

"Bucking Into The Teeth Of The Gale" - The Henry B. Smith

U.S. Navy P-3 Orion aircraft at Marquette County Airport prior to starting search effort. Marquette Maritime Museum

Grand Island theory. It is important to realize the greatest amount of information concerning where the wreckage was found is from the newspapers. It is anecdotal rather than analytical.

The loss of the *Henry B. Smith* remains substantially unexplained, with only speculation to fill in the void. The tragic fact remains that the *Smith*, one of the staunchest steel vessels on the lakes, turned up missing in the great storm of November 1913. As a point of macabre coincidence, Captain Owen had previously sailed for a time on the steamer *Iosco* thereby seeing service on two of the lake's "went missing" ships. The *Iosco*, towing the barge *Olive Jeanette*, disappeared with all hands near the Huron Islands west of Marquette in a September 1905 storm. It isn't too much of a stretch to speculate the *Smith* may not be too distant from her.

The *Smith* story is far from over. Over the last 30 years numerous efforts have been made to solve the mysteries of her loss and location. All have failed. Untold hours of side scan sonar work came up empty. Back tracking the wreckage fields using known wind speeds and direction computing the data with drift analysis software programs also failed. In 1987 the U.S. Navy even used a P-3 Orion submarine hunting aircraft in a search effort. The P-3s with their highly sophisticated magnetic anomaly detection (MAD) equipment are capable of locating Russian submarines (equipped with magnetic shielding hull coatings) hiding deep under the northern ice pack but couldn't find a 525-foot steel ore carrier filled with rich iron ore in Lake Superior. Go figure. A second Navy effort was made with the *USS Defender*. Charged and equipped to locate and neutralize enemy sea based mines, she seemed an ideal candidate to find the steamer. The *Defender* was on the Great Lakes as part of a Navy recruiting tour and used the *Smith* search as an opportunity to flex her search capability. She also failed to find the wreck. Go figure again.[xxv]

The USS Defender. *The MCM (mine-counter mine) vessel was unable to find the* Smith. *USN*

Regardless of past failures efforts continue to find and solve one of the great mysteries of the Great Lakes, the wreck of the *Henry B. Smith* remains "went missing".

C'EST LE GUERRE - THE *INKERMANN* AND *CERISOLES*[i]

Although all of the vessels in this book "went missing" for reasons not clearly understood, the most inexplicable losses were the double tragedy of the French Navy minesweepers *Inkermann* and *Cerisoles* on Lake Superior. To this day their fate remains one of the grand mysteries of the Great Lakes.

But how did two French Navy ships get to Lake Superior? The War was in Europe, not the Great Lakes. During the height of World War I European shipyards were going full blast with war construction. Merchant ships replacing those lost to German U-Boats, patrol craft to protect convoys, repair to British capital ships hammered in the great battle of Jutland, tugs and submarines, all were keeping shipyards choked with work. North American yards stepped in to fill the breach.

Minesweepers were critically short in the European Theater. Mine warfare, the laying of massive minefields to deny enemy use of the sea and particularly blocking sea approaches to ports and rivers increased tremendously during the war. Like the submarine, mines started the conflict as a weapon whose potential for destruction was grossly undervalued by traditional naval officers. Their effectiveness was quickly realized and soon there were millions in use and "sweeping" them, or clearing paths for ship traffic became a vital job. During peacetime Allied navies built large numbers of "capital ships," great battleships and battle cruisers awing the general public with their size and powerful guns. The more impressive the battleships, the greater the guarantee of more money to build bigger and better ones. Once the war started and powerful battleships started to sink after running into a very cheap mine, and critical merchant shipping plunged to the bottom for the same reasons, the call went out for the unglamorous little minesweepers. And there were hardly any since the navies only purchased the flashy capital ships, not the ugly, dirty little working ships. Procuring minesweepers as well as other small patrol craft became critical to the war. The big battleships were forced to largely idle the war away in port, too valuable to be risked to shell, torpedo or lowly mine while every day the "small boys" battled the enemy as well as the unforgiving and treacherous sea.

Although the records are fragmentary at best it seems the Manitowoc Shipbuilding Company in Manitowoc, Wisconsin was initially approached to build 12 minesweepers for the French Navy. For reasons yet unclear but we can assume fully committed U.S. shipyards, the company reached an agreement with Canadian Car and Foundry to do the actual construction work. The U.S. company also apparently provided some technical expertise but likely only limited on-site supervision.[ii]

Canadian Car and Foundry didn't have a shipyard but they did have an idle railcar plant at Fort William, on western Lake Superior. The facility was hardly well suited for conversion to a shipyard. A major disadvantage was it's 500 yard distance from the Kaministiquia River (aka Kam River). Shipyards are normally on the water, for very good reasons! The major advantage was the steel fabrication equipment. Perhaps more of a problem than realized when the decision was made to convert it to shipbuilding was the lack of a reasonably skilled workforce. A little ingenuity could solve the distance from water problem but the lack of a skilled workforce was more difficult to overcome. At this point in the war skilled men were engaged in other factories and industries, or long since swept into military service. The best the company could do was hire whoever it could find from wherever it could find them with the expected very mixed results.

Regardless of the difficulty, the new shipyard went to work and the lead vessel *Naravin* was started in June 1918. The entire dozen ship contract was completed in a fast six months.

Without dry docks the boats were built on land and then moved as complete hulls to the Kam River for launching. Once the hull was finished two rail cradles were moved into position on either side of the hull and wedged to take up the weight. Using pulleys and wire rope the hull was slowly hauled out of the building shed by a yard locomotive and onto a transfer table for movement to a permanent marine railway and launching. When safely afloat the ship was quickly finished with the addition of decks, machinery, living quarters, superstructure, weapons, etc. The minesweepers were launched at roughly two-week intervals.[iii]

C'est Le Guerre - The Inkermann and Cerisoles

The Naravin *on her way to launching. She is on the tracks with her weight being carried by four railcar-like devices. Note the hull plates and other hardware in the foreground of the photo.* Author

The original yard contract called for a dozen minesweepers, each 143-feet in length, 22-1/2 feet in beam, 13-1/4 feet in depth and displacing 630 tons.[iv] Each was to have four watertight compartments and a speed of 12 to 12-1/2 knots.[v] Nine of them had triple expansion steam engines built by the Nordberg Manufacturing Company in Milwaukee and three made by Chicago's Marine Iron Works. In practical terms, there was only a slight difference between any of the ships or their engines. All were built to the same set of plans.[vi]

All were named in honor of various French military victories; *Naravin*, *Mantoue*, *Saint Georges*, *Leoben*, *Palestro*, *Lutzen*, *Seneff*, *Sebastapol*, *Malakoff*, *Bautzen*, *Inkermann* and *Cerisoles*.[vii]

Canadian Car and Foundry Company, often just called "Can Car" manufactured railway and urban transportation rolling stock, ships, and later airplanes. The company was created in 1909 with the amalgamation of the nation's three largest railway rolling stock manufacturers. Starting with foundries, lumber mills and fabrication plants in Quebec and the Maritimes, the company moved into steel body casting and construction. It also quickly purchased the Montreal Steel Works of Longue Pointe, Quebec, and the Ontario Iron and Steel Company of Welland, Ontario, reorganizing them into the Canadian Steel Foundries Limited, the largest steel casting producer in Canada. By World War I the company had also purchased a foundry in Brantford and erected a fabrication plant in Fort William, Ontario.

WENT MISSING REDUX

By the 1920s the company's operations ranged to steel production, shipbuilding, and manufacturing luxury wooden railway cars, steel passenger and sleeper cars, freight rolling stock, and electric streetcars. It provided rail and urban transportation needs not only in Canada but also the United States, Brazil, and much of southern Africa. With the coming of World War II, the company further diversified into aircraft, bus, and motor coach manufacture. In 1955 it was gobbled up by the aircraft company A.V. Roe Canada Limited, which in turn closed most of the rolling stock plants. When British-based Hawker Siddeley Limited in turn acquired A.V. Roe Canada more steel plants were closed and the company focused on building aviation and urban transportation systems. In 1973 operations were organized into the Urban Transportation Development Corporation Limited and in 1992 acquired by the Bombardier Group. What makes this web of corporate history interesting is somewhere in the various takeovers, closings and acquisitions company records pertaining to the construction of the minesweepers were apparently lost. Missing records means speculation and that can lead to lots of misinformation.[viii]

As the minesweepers were completed they were assembled into groups and sent east to Montreal. After final preparations, it was planned they would cross the Atlantic to France and take their place in the war fleet.

At 11:15 a.m. Saturday, November 23, 1918 "Captain" Lieutenant Leclerc, the officer in charge of the last flotilla of three ships, *Sebastapol*, *Inkermann* and *Cerisoles*, gathered all the crews together and gave them a good "pep talk." He explained the importance of their working together to make the trip a success and the challenges faced. "La Belle" France needed these ships and regardless of the difficulty it was their job to get them there! Leclerc commanded the *Sebastapol* as well as the small flotilla.

The three ships were launched within eight days of each other. The *Cerisoles* was first, going in on September 25, 1918, the *Sebastapol* on the 30th and *Inkermann* on October 3. The *Navarin* was the first of the class to hit water, launching on July 29, 1918 and the *Inkermann* the last.[ix]

At noon the three ships, each manned by a 38-man French crew, left Fort William (today's Thunder Bay) together bound for the Soo and later Montreal. Crew breakdown included a captain, second officer, chief radio operator, master gunner, chief engineer, 23 sailors and 10 engineers.[x] The *Inkermann* was commanded by Captain Francois Mezou, the *Cerisoles* by Captain Etienne Deude and the *Sebastapol* by Captain Leclerc. The officers were considered competent. The title "captain" was in recognition of command, not military grade.[xi]

Each minesweeper was armed with two - four inch guns, one fore and one aft. Each ship was also radio equipped, a significant innovation for 1918 for

C'est Le Guerre - *The* Inkermann *and* Cerisoles

The minesweeper likely shown on or close to her departure from Fort William. Note the four-inch guns fore and aft and very small pilothouse. Author

such small ships. To assist the French officers who were clearly not familiar with the Great Lakes, each vessel carried an experienced Great Lakes pilot. Captain R. Wilson from Collingwood was in the *Inkermann* and Captain John W. Murphy from Buffalo in the *Cerisoles*. The *Sebastapol* carried two pilots, Captains Wood and McAvoy. They were all recommended by different agents of the Canada Steamship Lines and certainly competent. In the event the ships separated it was vital to have a pilot on each.[xii]

The three ships carried all of the typical nautical charts and bulletins needed as well a navigational equipment common for the time: a liquid main

The Inkermann *leading the* Cerisoles *downbound on Superior, a watercolor by Fr. Edward J. Dowling, S.J. Author Collection*

compass, chronometers, hand lead graduated in meters (it was a French ship after all), helix log, thermometer and aneroid barometer.[xiii]

There was a big rush to get the last three ships on their way. The Great Lakes would soon shut down for the winter and being "frozen" in Fort William or anywhere along the route to France was not desirable. On November 26 the Lower St. Lawrence River would close and any responsibility for navigation was left up to ships alone. The three vessels were apparently in all respects ready for sea so there was no reason for delay.[xiv]

At midnight on November 26 the *Sebastapol* arrived at the Soo. But she was alone, the *Inkermann* and *Cerisoles* having separated from her en route. After he "lost" the pair near Keweenaw Point Leclerc believed they either were behind him or somewhere ahead so he continued on for the Soo. Finding they hadn't arrived yet, he locked through and went on to Kingston, Ontario on Lake Ontario. The pair would catch up with him there. But they never even reached the Soo!

Although the war ended for practical purposes on November 11 with the signing of the Armistice, wartime sailing instructions, including secrecy, still applied, so there was a significant delay before an effective search for missing ships was started.

Finally on December 4 the Great Lakes Towing Company tugs *Bennett* and *Sarnia* stationed at Port Arthur went out to search for the pair. The *Bennett* looked along the north shore to Otter Head and the *Sarnia* covered the Isle Royale area. Later the *Sarnia* expanded her search as far as Houghton on the Keweenaw Peninsula. Other tugs cruised the Whitefish Point locale in the eastern lake. Freighters were also questioned by radio for any word of the pair. All gave negative reports. Since most freighters were not radio equipped this wasn't too surprising.

Once the lid of official secrecy came off, marine men began to reconstruct the fateful trip. The simple fact was twenty-four hours out from Thunder Bay the small fleet struck heavy weather accompanied by thick snow. At this point the *Sebastapol*, which was leading the group, lost sight of the *Inkermann* and *Cerisoles*.

A letter from a sailor on the *Sebastapol*, Marius Mollor, sheds some light on the storm. He wrote he had his lifebelt on, the lifeboat prepared and had "…already given himself up to God." He said about 11 o'clock a wave struck the ship almost submerging it and only the coolness of the captain averted disaster. He wrote, "I will never forget my experience on Lake Superior on the night of November 23-24."[xv] Mollor's letter wasn't unlike a letter from the radio operator of the *Seneff* sailing from Port Arthur on November 1 and finally reaching Montreal on the 30th. He reported a very rough crossing of

C'est Le Guerre - The **Inkermann** *and* **Cerisoles**

The Sneff *shown later in her life as a fishing trawler. Author*

Lake Erie on the 24th. "At 10:30 p.m. a big wave struck the stern of our ship. We were all in our bunks at the time but soon up on deck. The boat took water. We expected disaster. The boat stood on end and tossed around for nearly an hour. We have to have much repair work done to the boat before we can go out on the ocean."[xvi]

Captain Leclerc, in an interview during the subsequent search for the missing boats, described the *Sebastapol's* movements during the height of the gale. The wind was screaming from the southwest and forced the small fleet to head into it until they came up to the Keweenaw Point and were forced to turn northeast. The *Sebastapol* made the turn. By this time the storm had opened several of her seams and she had to constantly run her bilge pumps to stay ahead of the water. The engineroom was partially flooded and much debris was in the hold and in danger of fouling the engine.

It was at this point Leclerc lost sight of the *Inkermann* and *Cerisoles*. In later statements he implied he "lost" the two at the point of turning.

The U.S. Coast Guard combed the south shore of the lake looking for the missing twins as well as the area between Eagle Harbor and Manitou Island. Passing steamers were also questioned but none reported any clues. As in every mystery, rumors raged rampant. One said they were safe in Port Coldwell on the north shore. Another had the steamer *Midland Prince* sighting them safe at Richardson Harbor about 15 miles south of Otter Head. All proved false. The *Midland Prince* rumor started when a sailor mentioned in passing to a lock worker at the Soo that they were (in his opinion) likely at Otter Head. Apparently the *Midland Prince* spotted a strange light "flashing" at Richardson Harbor. As there is no lighthouse there, some of the crew believed it must therefore be the missing boats. After reflection it was realized later the light was likely from a searching tugboat. Regardless, the lock worker relayed the "news" to a reporter, who in the best traditions of his muckraking "profession" ran with the story even embellishing it to claim the crews were alive and starving. It's nice to know reporting back then was just as bad as it is today. Thus hope was raised only to be dashed when the facts were determined.[xvii]

Three days earlier Benjamin Truedell, the Grand Marais Coast Guard Station keeper, received a telegram from district headquarters directing him to make special beach patrols looking for clues to the lost minesweepers. Truedell of course telegrammed back he would do so and included the following. "At 7:00 p.m. December 1, small peculiar unknown steamer came close under land from N.W. and proceeded downbound. At same time and date a small unknown steamer from N.W. course came close under land at 295 (author's note: 295 was the Coast Guard station number) was warned off and proceeded down the lake. The wind was S.E. 36 miles, cloudy. At midnight a velocity at Whitefish Point of 48 miles existed with thick snow."[xviii]

Coast Guardsmen searched the south shore for clues to the losses. Author

C'est Le Guerre - The **Inkermann** *and* **Cerisoles**

Meanwhile Captain Leclerc returned from Kingston to take personal charge of the search for his missing ships. When he arrived at the Soo on the afternoon of December 5 he was met at the train station by a U.S. Navy Lieutenant Commander who assured him of the fullest cooperation of the American government. A representative of the Canadian Grand Trunk Railroad greeted him at his hotel, suggesting he embark immediately on the large passenger ship *S.S. Huronic*. The company delayed her departure for Fort William on the expectation he may want to use her to search the north shore. Leclerc thanked the railroad but considered her too large for his needs and he felt it vital to coordinate all of the search efforts rather than hurry off on his own.

Leclerc developed three hypotheses:

1. The ships foundered near Manitou Island.
2. They were lost on the south shore after passing Manitou Island in the vicinity of Grand Marais to Whitefish Bay.
3. After running before the storm they were cast ashore between Otter Head and Gargantua on the north shore.

The American Coast Guard was checking the Manitou area and had coastal beach patrols checking most of the south shore too so hypotheses 1 and 2 were covered. Regular steamer traffic was looking out for floating wreckage so that aspect was covered too. Fort William tugs swept Isle Royale on the unlikely chance the missing ships were there. The north shore was the only unresolved problem and he would have to personally handle it.

Leclerc was likely shocked to learn the Canadian government was virtually useless in providing assistance. Not only did it not have a ship he could use to search the north shore of the lake but there were no telegraph lines between the north shore light stations and any central point and only a private telephone to Michipicoten Island. The coast could only be reached by rail at two points otherwise it required a 60-mile dogsled trip through the winter wilderness. Neither was there a road along the coast and the lakeside was virtually deserted after November 1.[xix] Any search effort was strictly up to him. The Canadian government would be of no help.

Using the tug *Frank Weston*, he departed the Soo on December 9 to search the area around the north shore and Michipicoten Island. He wanted to charter the big 140-foot tug *Reliance* but it was unavailable forcing him to use the small 65-foot *Weston*. She only came with two crew and very minimal quarters providing little chance for rest en route. Worse perhaps was her very slow 8-knot cruising speed. The only advantage was cost, $75 a day versus $350 for the *Reliance*. But as the old expression goes, "beggers can't be

WENT MISSING REDUX

choosers" and with time dwindling away, he took the small tug and headed out into the lake.

Leclerc spent six days scouring the area covering several hundred miles fighting rough seas, iced in harbors and generally miserable weather, finding nothing. He did a remarkably thorough job but the "coast was clear." By the time he returned to the Soo he abandoned all hope for finding the ships unharmed or any of the crew alive. The *Weston* was the last boat down the locks before closing for the year. He telegraphed his sad report to the French Naval Commission at Port Arthur.[xx]

The Great Lakes Towing Company tugs from Port Arthur that were searching since December 4 also returned to port without finding a single clue to the missing ships.

Lieutenant Kerrieau, the inspector for the French Naval Commission supervising the construction work finally publicly took a pessimistic view of the missing ships on December 6. Previously he was always optimistic they would be found but after receiving Leclerc's telegram reporting his failure to locate them he was crushed. When reporters asked if he had given up hope, he just shrugged his shoulders.[xxii]

Later Leclerc wrote, likely with chagrin, "The results of this search do not allow us to determine the place, date and cause of the disappearance of the *Inkermann* and the *Cerisoles*!"[xxiii]

The first real potential clue was discovered on Friday December 6 when a patrolling Coast Guardsman at Grand Marais, Michigan found a new life ring washed up on the lonely shore. Although it was not marked as to vessel or painted, it did have the legend, "Manufactured by the Freysing Cork Company, Toronto, Canada, approved May 8, 1918, W.E. Marine, Buoyancy 32 pounds." The next day small pieces of broken, freshly painted and new matched lumber came ashore in the same area. There was doubt the wreckage was from the minesweepers however.[xxiv] The discovery of the yawl from the *Cerisoles* several days later by the Coast Guard beach patrol from Two-Heart River 25 miles west of Whitefish Point was damning. The yawl was painted gray and *Cerisoles* was emblazoned across each bow. Keeper Otto Frieke had also received a telegram warning of the missing ships so was well aware of the importance of discovery. Receiving the news by telegram Leclerc quickly headed for the area with a representative from Canadian Car. The trip was very arduous. The pair ended up spending a long night at Seney, Michigan, a lumber town whistle stop in the middle of nowhere. Snow was deep in the woods and the following day it took them seven hours by dog sled to reach Grand Marais, a distance of only 25 miles. After looking at the life ring and other wreckage the pair concluded it wasn't from the minesweepers. Their

C'est Le Guerre - The **Inkermann** *and* **Cerisoles**

rings were all painted red and white and inscribed with the ship's name. The wood was also from some other ship, not theirs. The pair never actually examined the yawl.[xxv] Likely they looked at the dogsleds and considered the value of bouncing another 20 miles through the forest to the Two-Heart station and decided they would just use the telephone. After speaking with the Coast Guardsmen they concluded there wasn't any doubt the yawl was from the *Cerisoles*. It was clear too there was no indication it was ever used, likely breaking off the davits when the ship sank.[xxvi]

The French Navy officially gave up all hope on December 15 and began the difficult process of notifying the next of kin, for the sailors as well as Great Lakes pilots.[xxvii]

But what happened to the ships and men? How did two brand new and supposedly seaworthy vessels literally disappear?

Examining the *Inkermann - Cerisoles* case more closely, a number of interesting facets come to light.

Many of the "sailors" on all three ships were sailors in name only having recently been transferred from the Army as unfit for further combat service in the trenches. Sailors are not created by government fiat. It takes years of experience to become competent. How well would the instant seamen have performed in a storm?

Although all the vessels carried radios, the operators by Leclerc's admission, were more students than skilled operators. In the midst of a roaring Superior gale would they have been able to communicate effectively?

In the years following the disaster a number of theories were advanced. One claims the *Inkermann* and *Cerisoles* struck Superior Shoal. The shoal wasn't discovered until 1929 and a mere 18 miles north of the steamer track from Thunder Bay to the Soo. However Leclerc's own statements placed the three ships just off Keweenaw Point, more than 50 miles southeast of the shoal. In the light of Leclerc's report, the shoal theory lacks credibility.

Another theory claims when the vessels were built they were temporarily pegged together with wood dowels pending final assembly. During the hectic last days at the yard, some of the wooden pegs were never removed and during the height of the gale the pegs failed. Many marine historians and vessel men of the time find this theory absurd.

A Mr. P. Corkindale (McCorkendale?), the Lloyd's surveyor at the Fort William yard stated he and four French inspectors were present constantly during construction and the ships were well built. He did make the point that they were built without many of the finishing touches normally put in during peacetime but this had nothing to do with their seaworthiness or strength.[xxviii] Leaving out the frills was typical for wartime construction.

The Peary *on the way to the North Pole expedition. Note the seaplanes carried on the aft deck.* Author

As further evidence of the craft's basic sturdiness one of the dozen, the *Bautzen*, was later renamed the *S.S. Peary* and used on the 1925 MacMillan - McDonald - Byrd - Arctic Expedition. The *Peary* often broke heavy ice, frequently lifting her bows into 100-ton blocks and splitting them. During the expedition she encountered several severe storms, one of which sank a Danish Naval vessel at Gothaad, Greenland. The *Peary*, seaworthy enough to brush aside the wild polar seas, was able to rescue the Dane's crew.[xxix]

Although partially refitted in the Brooklyn Navy Yard prior to departure for the Arctic, she was essentially the same vessel as built in Fort William. During the expedition she was often heavily overloaded, carrying not only three disassembled airplanes as deck cargo but also 60 tons of coal, half piled on deck. Every available space was stacked with expedition supplies, including spare aircraft engines, barrels of aviation gas and four extra boats. She was so heavily laden her forward portholes were constantly underwater! In fact when she stopped at Labrador for refueling the captain ordered steel plates welded over the portholes in recognition of danger. Fishermen who watched her sail off into the stormy northern seas later said they never expect-

C'est Le Guerre - The **Inkermann** *and* **Cerisoles**

ed to see her again! At one point she struck an uncharted shoal, running on so hard she listed 40 degrees to port. A heavy sea was running and the *Peary* pounding hard on the rocks. Regardless, with the help of a second ship and rising tide she was able to get off without serious damage. During her return from the Arctic she survived an especially violent storm. One of her men remembering she was almost completely underwater, the huge waves shattering several main cabin portholes. Water flooded cabins and below decks.[xxx] The point is the *Peary* (old *Bautzen*) was a very strong and seaworthy vessel. There is no evidence she had a major rebuild from the time of her launching to steaming north with the expedition.

The expedition was under the leadership of famed Arctic explorer Donald MacMillian and Zenith Radio Company founder and owner Eugene McDonald. Lt. Commander Richard Byrd of the U.S. Navy commanded the Naval aviation component. The expedition is best remembered today as being the first to use fixed wing aircraft in the high Arctic as part of a scientific exploration as well as short wave radio for long range communications. Previously only long wave radio was used which was limited to night only and of much shorter range. The short wave sets were smaller and messages were regularly passed between the expedition and stations in the U.S. Radios were also used for the first time on single engine amphibian aircraft. The initial testing of the airborne radios was done on Lake Michigan adding another Great Lakes link to the expedition.[xxxi]

The *Bautzen's* career involved more than just being an Arctic expedition ship. From her original French ownership she passed to an M. Goddard (*Rowena*) in New York, then to Donald B. MacMillan in 1925 for expedition use (*Peary*), then to the U.S. Army Corps of Engineers for use as a Lake Survey boat, to a G.L. Allen in Dearborn, Michigan and finally to Pulsifer

The Bautzen *later morphed into the* Peary *and saw North Pole adventure. Author*

WENT MISSING REDUX

The U.S. Lake Survey ship Peary. *NOAA*

Brothers in Halifax as a fishing boat. She foundered in a gale 60 miles off St. Pierre, Canada in 1961.[xxxii]

As evidenced by the *Peary's* performance the 12 vessels built at Port Arthur were a group characterized by excellent seaworthiness and strength. Especially recognize that the *Bautzen* (*Peary*) was one of the batch built with the *Inkermann* and *Cerisoles* (although she didn't sail with the *Inkermann* and *Cerisoles*). Any construction or design faults in one ship should have been common to all three.

None of the dozen minesweepers ever reached France. The war was over and all were disposed of as surplus. Their subsequent careers were varied; fishing, salvage, Canadian Government, one was seized trying to run bootleg booze into the U.S. in 1926 and two, the old *Mantoue* and *St. Georges*, finally went to war when they were taken over by the Canadian Navy during World War II serving as anti-submarine yachts.[xxxiii] The *St. Georges*, renamed *Dorothy Duke*, was requisitioned in 1940 and returned in 1946. Most of her time was spent in at Trinidad in the West Indies. Armament was usually just depth charges and perhaps one or two small caliber guns added later.[xxxiv]

What then did happen to the two missing ships? That they foundered is undoubted (unless one was prone to believe in alien abduction of ships and crews). The questions are when and where did they founder? Why will likely not be answered until discovery when hopefully the secret can be pulled out of their wreckage.

We can probably accept Leclerc's story of running into the teeth of the seas southwest to Keweenaw Point as being true. After all a Great Lakes pilot caught on Superior with a strong southwest gale would logically run for the shelter of the south shore and Keweenaw Point is the closest location. From his comments we can deduce the ships were having a tough time of it, regardless of their staunch construction. After all, Superior swallowed the

C'est Le Guerre - The Inkermann *and* Cerisoles

729-foot *Edmund Fitzgerald* with all hands in November 1975. What was a pair of 143-foot minesweepers compared to her?

If the *Sebastapol* opened her seams, partially flooding her engine room and taking green water over the bow, the *Inkermann* and *Cerisoles* must have been in comparable condition. Add to the situation the inexperienced crew, half of whom were probably seasick and we have a very desperate situation. Furthermore if we believe contemporary news accounts, it appears Leclerc was actually only a lieutenant in the French Navy. The title "captain" was purely honorary in recognition of his command of a ship. If a lieutenant was in charge of the fleet, what type of "experienced officer" had charge of the two subordinate vessels? Certainly the French officers were not highly experienced mariners, high seas or Great Lakes. While we can assume they were competent, there isn't any real proof of it.[xxxv]

With Keweenaw Point coming up fast the *Sebastapol* timed the critical turn correctly, completed it and survived. Is it not possible the *Inkermann* and *Cerisoles*, desperately beset by flooding holds and leaking seams and rivets, with less experienced officers and seasick crews, failed in their turns and rolled in the heavy waves? If that happened, there would be precious little wreckage, the capsized vessels sinking immediately.

One argument of loss claims the ships were unstable due to the weight of the two 4 inch naval guns mounted topside. This certainly could be true but remember during the *Bautzen's* Arctic work (as *Peary*) she too carried an immense amount of deck cargo, much of it offering considerable wind resistance such as vertically boxed aircraft wings. She survived so why not the *Inkermann* and *Cerisoles*? Perhaps the difference was crew competence. The *Peary* had a professional crew and master mariner as captain in contrast to her sister's scratch crews.

There is also the possibility the *Inkermann* and *Cerisoles* collided during a period of low visibility. However most masters prefer to keep well clear of other boats even in good weather. Although they sailed in a group, they certainly weren't steaming in formation. The Great Lakes pilots loathed being near another boat. The fear of collision is a mark of a prudent commercial mariner in contrast to the more risky approach often taken by naval officers. This doesn't mean naval officers are inherently dangerous, but the nature of war at sea often requires steaming at full speed in very close formation. For example, motor torpedo boats or destroyers delivering an attack.

A point of analysis often missed is the lack of bodies. With the 78 French sailors plus the two Great Lakes pilots, it is surprising a considerable number of bodies weren't found immediately after the losses or frozen in shore ice in the spring. This would indicate the vessels sank suddenly, capsizing without

WENT MISSING REDUX

warning, not even leaving enough time for a man to put on a lifebelt. Neither were there any reports of lifebelts found along the coast or in floating debris fields leading to the conclusion they were still in their storage lockers and not distributed to the crew. Without lifebelts the men sank to the bottom and as the old saying goes, Lake Superior doesn't give up her dead!

But did she give up at least some? There is a story that in 1934 several fishermen discovered two skeletons on the shore at Michipicoten Island's West Sand Bay. Reportedly they wore the remnants of French Navy uniforms and had French I.D. tags. The fisherman put the remains in a wood fish box and buried it above the water line. No marker was placed on the grave feeling to do so was to invite ghoulish curiosity seekers. The I.D. tags were sent to the "authorities" but as the fishermen reportedly never heard any response the whole incident just "went away." While this is a great story there are a couple of issues with it. Could bodies and their uniforms have survived 16 years on an open beach on the shores of Lake Superior? How did the fishermen know they were French uniforms, especially after 16 years? Or even one year? The

Was the story true about the skeletons of French sailors being found on Michipicoten Island? Edward Pusick

C'est Le Guerre - The Inkermann *and* Cerisoles

distance from the last sighting of the ships was about 75 miles to the west. While this may seem to be a long way for a body to drift, it isn't unheard of on Lake Superior. When the big steamer *Henry B. Smith* sank somewhere near the Keweenaw in November 1913, one of the few bodies was found the following spring near Michipicoten Island. If the skeletons were sailors from the missing ships, they were the only remains reported found.[xxxvi]

If the three minesweepers survived their Lake Superior sojourn and the war not ended on November 11, it would have been interesting to speculate as to what kind of conditions they would have faced on the Atlantic crossing. The North Atlantic is never easy and winter conditions on that stretch of wild ocean are abominable.

Any loss like the two minesweepers ignites the wildest of theories. One of the best claims a German U-boat was in Lake Superior and even though it was two weeks after the armistice ending the war, torpedoed them both. The submarine then either returned to the ocean without being seen or sank into the depths of Superior by some accident. Of course to reach Lake Superior the sub either magically appeared or managed to sneak through the St. Lawrence River, Welland Canal and Soo Locks. I didn't say the theory was in the least believable just that it is "out there."[xxxvii]

What exactly actually happened to the missing *Inkermann* and *Cerisoles* will perhaps never be known. But with the continuous improvement of various search technologies their dead hulls will someday be found. Regardless of future certainty, at this moment the lone clue to one of the lake's greatest mysteries was the forlorn yawl on the beach at Two-Heart.

ADDENDUM TO *INKERMANN* AND *CERISOLES*

The lay reader will be satisfied with the previous piece on the *Inkermann* and *Cerisoles*. The true shipwreck aficionado will want more, thus the following previously unpublished material. While this data does not substantially change the previous information, it does provide another layer of speculation, of what could have happened.

The Minesweepers

Understanding the process and problems of minesweeping can help the reader gain a better appreciation of the vital role these craft were designed to fill.

During World War I mines were anchored to the bottom of the sea and allowed to float at various depths by a wire cable from the anchor to the mine. The size of a minefield could vary from a dozen or so mines, for example laid by a German submarine off a busy British port, to a million or more in a huge

Went Missing Redux

barrier established by the Allies to deny massive areas of the English Channel to German naval units.

Minesweepers had the job of clearing either the entire minefield or cutting a channel through it for other ships to use. During World War I all of the mines were "contact" mines designed to detonate when struck by a ship. They were usually round shaped with a number of "horns" or contacts projecting outward. Strike the horn and the mine explodes sinking the ship.

World War I minesweepers used mechanical systems to clear mines, thus the term "mine sweeping." The sweep was a serrated wire cable dragged through the water behind the minesweeper and intended to cut the mooring cable of an anchored mine. When the sweep wire strikes the mine anchor cable it rubs along it until the friction cuts it or it is severed by a special cutter at the end of the sweep wire. A planning device keeps the sweep wire and cutter at a predetermined distance and angle from the vessel. This is not dissimilar to the devices used to keep large fishing trawl nets open or sport fishing planning boards. Various depressor devices hold the sweep cable down and a surface float marks the bitter end. Sweeps can be employed from either side of the vessel. One "sweep" by a minesweeper generally cleared 150-yard wide channel.

Once the mine anchor cable is cut, the mine floats to the surface and in theory is exploded by gunfire. Some minesweepers carried designated marksmen to do the job. Others let all crewmen take a shot at it. Hitting a mine bouncing around in a sea isn't easy to do. Of course the closer you went, the bigger the target and greater danger from the blast when it finally exploded.

German mines were especially effective devices. In fact the British "reverse engineered" a captured German mine to build their first reliable contact mine. By war's end a mere 43,000 German mines accounted for nearly 500 British merchant ships, 44 warships and 235 auxiliaries, including a number of submarines. Since mines were very cheap to manufacture, it was a good cost - kill ratio.

Some folks today are surprised the French minesweepers built in Fort William were steel hulled as at present fiberglass or wood (in some combination) is more common. However during World War I magnetically actuated mines were not used so steel hulls were standard. The magnetic mine lies in wait on the sea bottom until a ship passes overhead distorting the normal earth's magnetic field enough to trigger the explosion.

Because the war was the first time mines were used in such massive numbers and sophistication and sweeping them became so critical, the Allies were scraping the barrel to find boats suitable for use as minesweepers. Since

Addendum To Inkermann *and* Cerisoles

A World War I German contact mine ready to deploy. The rectangular piece contains the anchor and cable tethering the mine to the sea bottom. Author

a fishing trawler design worked well, a large open stern and usually equipment aboard to stream the cables, governments requisitioned hundreds from the commercial fishing fleets. As Naval crews were equally scarce, in some instances the civilians were taken with the boats! The fishermen were usually not the most willing sailors or enthusiastic about their new job! The traditional trawler design also offered excellent sea-keeping ability, an important consideration for the mission.

Minesweeping was very dangerous. The ships have to proceed slowly and in line to be assured of clearing a safe path. It's like mowing grass with a series of lawn mowers all taking their paths from the cutting of the machine ahead. Keeping in a tight formation also makes the minesweepers easy targets. During the Gallipoli Campaign in World War I the British lost a number civilian manned minesweepers to Turkish gunfire from shore. Other minesweepers were destroyed when they struck mines. Remember, while most ships are supposed to stay clear of mines, minesweepers by mission, have to charge right in to their midst.

WENT MISSING REDUX

Sea mines have been around a long time. The first recorded use dates from the Ming Dynasty in China in the 14th Century. Every major conflict since saw mine warfare and constant technological improvement, including the American Revolution, Crimean War, American Civil War and Russo-Japanese War. Since mines were (and are) primarily a poor man's weapon, it was usually the underdog employing most of them.[i]

Wartime Construction on the Lakes

It wasn't an anomaly small warships like the minesweepers were being built at a backwater like Fort William. Many Great Lakes shipyards were busy with war construction of both combat vessels and ocean-going merchantmen. Of course the East Coast yards got the greatest amount of work. That relegated to the Great Lakes was constrained by the size of the Soo Locks for Lake Superior and Welland Canal for the lower lakes.

For example, the British ordered 112 - 500-ton "*Eagle*" class patrol boats from U.S. yards. All of them ever built were on the Great Lakes by Ford using his famous assembly line techniques giving rise the moniker "Ford boats." Only 60 were finished and nearly all of those after the war.[ii]

A number of 110-foot wooden subchasers were built on the Great Lakes for the French, many in small Ohio shipyards like the Rocky River Dry Dock Company in Rocky River and Mathew Boat Company in Port Clinton. Supposedly when the French sailors arrived to take them home the local ladies freely entertained the brave mariners.[iii] The French sailors had to be more exciting than the typical Ohio farm boys!

Merchant ships were also built on the Great Lakes for the war. One specialized design was called the "Lake" class. Relatively small for ocean going ships at 2,300 tons, they were designed to fit through the comparatively small Welland Canal locks. Eventually 68 saw service under the U.S. War Shipping Board.[iv] British merchant vessels were also built on the lakes with work done at virtually all of the big U.S. and Canadian shipyards.[v]

While the French minesweepers were being built at a converted railcar factory in Fort William a proper shipyard in Port Arthur just to the north was also turning out ships for the war effort. The Western Dry Dock Company built a large laker plus several ocean-going freighters for both the Canadian Government and British Admiralty. Before the war ended it also launched a number of armed naval trawlers for both entities. Some sources describe the trawlers as minesweepers. Since the physical characteristics of both ships are the same less equipment provided, they could have served either mission. Technically designated at "TR" they were copies of the British "Castle" class. Fourteen were built at the Port Arthur Shipbuilding Company yard. And

Addendum To Inkermann *and* Cerisoles

another 31 elsewhere on the lakes. Sometimes the British (Canadian minesweepers) built at Port Arthur and French ones at Fort William are confused. Virtually none saw war service and many were sold as fishing trawlers. A number were seconded to the Royal Navy during World War II. The Western Dry Dock Company became the Port Arthur Shipbuilding Company in 1916.[vi]

World War II of course saw very heavy shipbuilding in both Canadian and American yards. With some exception all the World War I classes were built. Submarines were the new addition but that is certainly another story.

French Naval Attaché Investigation

The loss of two naval vessels complete with crews was not something to be easily forgotten about, at least not at first. The French went far beyond the relatively simple investigation Leclerc performed.

Lieutenant de Chevigne, the Assistant French Naval attaché in Washington was dispatched to Canada to investigate the disaster. Chief Engineer Triqueneaux, who oversaw the technical aspects of the building program for the French Navy assisted him with advice and support.[vii]

Meeting with the French Consul General in Montreal de Chevigne ran into his own problems working with the Canadians concerning the investigation. While the Canadian government appeared very cooperative to the French officer and even willing to provide the assistance of the Wreck Commissioner from Ottawa, there was no substance to the offer. The Wreck Commissioner was required to immediately carry out an investigation on the Pacific coast so he was unable to help in a timely manner. Apparently no offer was made for another official to stand in for the Wreck Commissioner nor did he have an assistant. Like Leclerc, if he wanted something done, the French officer would have to do it himself. In the end the lieutenant and his team proceeded without Canadian government assistance.[viii]

To determine if there was anything obviously wrong with the ships as a class, the investigators met with Great Lakes pilots who had experience with the rest of the ships. However none of the pilots they interviewed actually made the trip down from Thunder Bay and only worked the boats in rivers and harbors. They had no experience with them on the open lake in difficult conditions. As a group though, they agreed a large movement of the helm could cause the ships to take on a marked list and in heavy weather it could be fatal.

The team interviewed a Mr. Parks, the vice-president of Canadian Car and Foundry and a number of his colleagues in the company's Montreal office. Responding to the French officer's questions, Parks opined the only plausible explanation for the loss was a collision between the two ships. It was unlikely both would have been lost with all hands on the same night by foundering without being able to either radio for help or at least firing distress rockets, either of which would have alerted the *Sebastapol* or someone on shore. The problem with his hypothesis was it first assumed foggy weather allowing the two ships to collide however according to the pilots on the *Sebastapol* fog was not present. Second, it assumed the *Sebastapol* was close by the *Inkermann* and *Cerisoles* at the time of loss. It was conceivable the ships could have collided during a rescue attempt but more on this later.

Parks also claimed the French crews were of "inferior quality" which he based on comments from the French officers at Fort William as well as examples of ship handling problems. For example, the *Mantoue* collided with a ferryboat during delivery in spite of having 30 miles of clearance "on each side." On another vessel the Chief Engineer put the engine in full ahead rather than reverse as signaled from the bridge creating havoc. When mooring at a Fort William dock another of the ships had extreme difficulty avoiding a steamer moored nearby and finally one of the ships smashed into her dock. All of these "accidents" speak eloquently to a lack of crew training, experience and competence. Lieutenant de Chevigne held his tongue and didn't defend the crews. From his report it is evident he felt some indignation of Park's comments regarding French naval performance. Likely there was more truth in the comments than the French officer would admit. French pride is always easily bruised.[ix] It is fair to assume there was little time to train the crews, especially considering their non-maritime background. A lack of competence was the result.

The Lieutenant and his team next met with the two pilots from the *Sebastapol* at the little village of Merriton Junction near Niagara Falls. The meeting lasted about two and a half hours, long enough for a detailed and frank discussion. The pilots recalled the weather was fine when they left Fort William, a calm sea with a light southwest breeze. All went well until about 7:00 p.m. when the wind and sea began to increase. Ominously conditions slowly deteriorated until a full southwest gale was blowing.

The *Sebastapol* and by implication the *Inkermann* and *Cerisoles*, started to take on water and Lieutenant Leclerc changed course to head for land as quickly as possible. About 11:00 p.m. at a point off Copper Harbor the *Sebastapol* apparently fell into the trough of the sea and had difficulty climbing out. To the pilot's recollection the two following ships didn't have the same problem. Around 1:00 a.m. the lights of the *Inkermann* and *Cerisoles* disappeared. There was no fog.

Addendum To Inkermann *and* Cerisoles

About 2:00 a.m. the *Sebastapol* suddenly refused to obey her helm and made a complete circle before the crew was able to bring her back under control. An hour later she entered the channel between the tip of the Keweenaw and Manitou Island. At 4:30 a.m. there was more trouble with the helm and the wheel chains were unshackled and the ship steered by hand.

An hour later she headed for shelter at Bete Gris just inside the hook of the Keweenaw. The pilots said Leclerc expected to find the missing two ships anchored there but when they weren't he assumed they either had continued on without him or if still behind him, they would soon come around the point. One of the pilots, Mr. Hood told Leclerc they were "gone" but the Lieutenant refused to believe it, claiming they were still continuing down for the Soo.

Neither pilot made specific criticisms of the *Sebastapol* but did find her generally mediocre in handling. Although they discovered some water entering through defective riveting her stability didn't appear to be especially precarious. They considered the gale reasonably severe and mentioned much larger ships had already found shelter from it.

It is interesting Leclerc didn't consult the pilots as to his selected route. Clearly the French officer piloted his ship, which leads to the question of why the pilots were even aboard if he didn't consult them? Was it misplaced French pride?

Manitou Island Lighthouse. The captain of the Sebastopol *clearly saw it's powerful beam.* Author

WENT MISSING REDUX

The final question the lieutenant put to the pilots was would they do it again, same ship, same storm and same route. Both said yes, but only if they choose the route, the northern route, not Leclerc's direct course. More on this later.[x]

The attaché and his engineer finally met with Leclerc a week later in New York. While the questioning doesn't appear to be hostile, it certainly was pointed.

Leclerc told the lieutenant that once he cleared Passage Island at the north tip of Isle Royale he decided to run directly for the Soo rather than follow the northern or southern routes. Leclerc reasoned the north route was only an advantage if he ran close enough to land to be able to use it as a shelter. There are few ports and roadsteads along the route and most anchorages are unmarked by lights. The few that are lit aren't reliable which meant he could only enter during daylight. Stating the lights weren't "reliable" was a damning accusation against the Canadian government. If a light has to be anything, its reliable. Given the generally cavalier fashion the government treated it's lights, there is a considerable amount of truth in his comment.

He said the southern route could be used only in good weather or with winds from southeast to southwest. It's advantage is it is well lit with harbors every 30 miles or so. He saw the disadvantage as having to cross the "cemetery of Lake Superior," the stretch of stormy water between Copper Harbor and Manitou Island.

The direct route, roughly 160 miles from Passage Island to Whitefish Point was the quickest. He also would never be more than 40 miles from land. Unless the weather was storming, he considered this the best route.

Remember though, he never consulted either pilot on his choice of course or explained his reasoning to them. In his defense, neither did they, at least according to Leclerc, object to his decision. Given his generally negative evaluation of the pilots, would he have listened to their suggestions anyway?

Apparently the folks at Fort William predicted an easy crossing for Leclerc with calm seas and light northwest winds. With such a good forecast he was soon downbound for the Soo. Perhaps they just wanted to be rid of him?

When the wind shifted to southwest about 6:15 p.m. he considered three options. He could come about for Isle Royale but there was no light at Rock Harbor preventing his entry at night. Siskiwit Bay had a light at Menagerie Island but offered only marginal shelter. He could run for the north shore but it was 60 miles distant and offered no shelter with a southwest gale. His only real option was head for the Keweenaw about 35 miles ahead. He therefore set course for Manitou Island at the tip of the Keweenaw Peninsula.

About 7:00 p.m. the ships were taking on water from the southwest seas, slopping over their starboard quarters. To counter the waves he swung to the

Addendum To Inkermann and Cerisoles

south intending to reach shelter along the coast between Copper Harbor and Agate Harbor as soon as possible. Once he was within five to ten miles of shore the waters should be quieter.

Shortly after his turn the storm increased in ferocity and short, sharp seas were slamming into the ships. The *Inkermann* and *Cerisoles* fell behind for some unknown reason and Leclerc duly decreased speed to 90 revolutions. Once both were back on station he went back to 100 revolutions although his speed was only four or five knots. All the boats were still taking on water. The bows slamming into the waves and deluges of Superior slopping back over the weather decks. Barrels of oil and grease stored on the stern constantly came loose and had to be repeatedly lashed down.

Leclerc claimed water entering through the boiler and engine room doors, deck seams and stern frames was only a nuisance for men below similar to the "permanent shower" the deck crew was getting on the open bridge. He didn't see the water as a serious problem.

Copper Harbor Light was sighted at 22:30 p.m. and a few minutes later Manitou Island Light was visible too. Both confirmed his dead reckoning navigation.

At 11:10 p.m. the helmsman "lost" control of the *Sebastapol* and she broached falling into the trough of the waves, portside down.[xi] Leclerc was not on the bridge at the time and blamed it on his pilots, saying they were in too much of a hurry to reach Copper Harbor. Another wave swamped her, flooding over the starboard rail, pushing her further under. The watch on deck were stunned and froze into inaction, the men below rushing from their quarters to find lifebelts. Leclerc swiftly ran from his quarters adjacent to the navigating cabin and grabbing the wheel signaled full speed ahead throwing her helm hard to port, climbing out of the trough and putting the waves on her stern. By the time he completed the maneuver her deck was flooded to the gunwales! After settling down on her new course the water slowly drained away. It was a near thing!

He ran northeast until midnight steering himself for part of the time, both to rest his demoralized crew and square things away on the bridge, which was thrown into chaos by the broaching. He also needed time for the engine room crew to recover not only from the broach but also the constant flooding. After turning the bridge over to his second in command he climbed down to the engine room to assess the situation for himself. With an inexperienced crew he needed to see what was really happening, unable to trust their judgment. A few minutes earlier a messenger from the chief engineer warned him there was so much water in the compartment they could lose the engine! Lelerc initially thought the situation was exaggerated but when he entered the compartment he saw it was serious indeed. Enough water entered through the deck, roof seams, bulkhead doors and stern that it was up to the top of the crankshafts. As the ship rolled and pitched, the water picked up all matter of debris including rags, bits of wood and planks blocking the bilge pump suction head. Perhaps worse, a piece of wood could easily jam the machinery. The engine room crew eventually straightened it all out and by midnight the compartment was clear of water and floating debris.

About midnight with his ship reasonably shipshape again, he swung back toward land. The seas were running very heavy with waves breaking at between 15 and 20 feet high. Going was difficult but between 2:00 a.m. and 2:30 a.m. he made it to within several miles of the shore and swung left to follow the coast to the Point. The wind had shredded his jib and the heavy canvas sail was beating violently. It was far too dangerous to try to haul it in.[xii] For reasons Leclerc didn't explain, the helm failed and the *Sebastapol* suddenly and inexplicably made a complete circle to port even though the helm control and servomotor were put "Hard Starboard." After considerable effort he managed to regain control and continued on towards the coast. "Servomotor" is a French term for a steering engine, which is a steam, electric or hydraulic power machine used to work the rudder and having it's valves or operating gear actuated by leads from the bridge. Think of it as a nautical variant of "power steering."

Leclerc said around 3:15 a.m. the *Sebastapol* entered the channel between Manitou Island and Keweenaw Point. At 4:50 a.m. the helm again locked up. He and his crew attempted to force it free with tackle but without success. Only by unshackling the wheel and steering by hand were they able to carry on, finishing by 5:30 a.m. Continuing around the Point the *Sebastapol* reached Bete Gris and anchoring in the relatively calm water at 7:30 a.m.

Leclerc reported he lost sight of the others about 11:10 p.m. when he broached and recovered placing the wind and seas astern. At the time the *Inkermann* was about 200 yards behind him and the *Cerisoles* 500-600 yards beyond the *Inkermann*. Neither followed his new course. Around midnight when he swung back for the coast he saw by their lights (red sidelights) they had turned northeastward. He assumed they were in calmer seas and heading for the Keweenaw Point passage. He estimated them to be at least a mile apart and judging from her two white lights, the most easterly was the *Inkermann*. The two white lights were an erroneous set on the part of the *Inkermann* but since they let Leclerc distinguish her from the *Cerisoles*, he didn't correct the mistake.

Between 12:30 and 1:00 a.m. the lights of the *Inkermann* and *Cerisoles* disappeared. He assumed both had swung away to round Keweenaw Point

Addendum To Inkermann *and* Cerisoles

thus were no longer visible. He didn't see any light signals, Coston flares or rockets indicating distress. With only one operator per boat maintaining a constant radio watch was impossible.

Leclerc emphasized when he broached he made certain to make no signal that could be construed to be distress or asking for help. Under the storm conditions any attempt to render aid would certainly cause the loss of the other vessel. Two boats couldn't lay alongside without fatal damage. It was impossible to launch lifeboats and the crews were far too inexperienced to manage them in the large breaking seas. He also felt the piecing cold would have been deadly for his men.

Communication between the ships was nearly nonexistent. When Leclerc made the flag signal "Is all well" between 6:00 - 7:00 p.m. the only acknowledgement came from the *Inkermann* and an acknowledgement isn't a reply, merely a confirmation she understands the signal. He didn't bother to signal his plan to head for the Keweenaw as they failed to reply to his early signal and he figured they would follow him anyway. Since he directed the radios not be used unless there was fog or they became separated, wireless wasn't an answer either.

According to Leclerc when the ships lost visual contact with him around 1:00 a.m. they should have kept a radio watch for the first half hour of each following hour for four hours. But since he assumed they safely rounded the Point and were at anchor behind it or enduring on for the Soo, he didn't initiate his watch. IF they had gone to a radio watch, the leader wasn't "on the air." The effect was he was no longer in command of his charges.

When he arrived at Bete Gris at 7:00 a.m. and didn't see the two ships he ordered his radio operator to start calling them off and on until the afternoon. There was no answer. Neither was he able to contact the Soo or Port Arthur to get a weather report. Considering the storm they went through Leclerc didn't think the lack of radio signals from the ships unusual. The operators were probably too tired and resting or their radios or aerials could have been damaged. But was it likely both ships had the same problem?

Since the Bete Gris anchorage was empty of his missing ships Leclerc concluded they had already passed and continued on for the south shore heading for a point between Big Bay Point and Granite Island. When he lost sight of the pair they appeared to be in relatively calm water close to shore. They must be continuing independently for the Soo.

Apparently Leclerc and his pilots finally had "words." He complained about the, "timid suggestions of my pilots who were more worried about their fate." (This strikes me as a very good reason to be very apprehensive!) Leclerc said he never worried about his own ship once, "I had mastered her movements!"[xiii]

Went Missing Redux

The *Sebastapol's* steering servomotor wasn't repaired until noon on the 24th. The wind was blowing strong west and he felt it imprudent to continue so he waited out the gale. Big freighters still coming in to shelter at Bete Gris reinforced his decision.

Considering later where the *Inkermann* and *Cerisoles* may have been lost he concluded either near Manitou Island or on a direct course for the south shore. The severe weather prevented him from going back into the teeth of seas to search around Manitou and scanning the south shore was just too big of a job for a single ship. He determined to press on to the Soo alone. But he had no reason to think they were in trouble.

If for any reason the pair lost control in the storm, perhaps suffering helm damage or engine failure, he believed they would certainly capsize immediately. The question of course is would both capsize at the same time and place and if so, where?

With no definite information on the missing ships, Leclerc decided to continue on for the Soo and ultimately Montreal. The experience during delivery of the previous ships showed normally all had suffered damage of some kind. With this in mind the policy was if one was damaged the others would continue on rather than be delayed. Damaged ships were instructed to put into the closest port and telegraph their situation to the Naval Attaché. The French were still planning to sail the minesweepers across the North Atlantic and wanted to do so as soon as possible so it was imperative to reach Montreal without delay. Leclerc also felt the *Sebastapol* didn't have the sea keeping qualities necessary to conduct a proper search anyway.

The *Sebastapol* finally left Bete Gris at 8:30 a.m. on the 25th, delaying longer than intended by the need to repair her anchor windlass. Apparently the stress of the storm loosened the steam piping requiring repacking and tightening joints. Leclerc decided to run east to Caribou Island both to check the east end of the lake for the missing ships and to allow a safer run to the Soo if the prevailing west northwest winds turned northeast and increased in force. He still was unable to get a wireless weather forecast.

When he locked through the Canadian Soo at 3:00 a.m. on the 26th, he asked the superintendent if the *Inkermann* and *Cerisoles* arrived earlier. Learning they didn't he asked to be informed by telegraph to Port Colbourne, the entrance to the Welland Canal, when they arrived. He still felt they were simply delayed. Leclerc continued on for Kingston and Montreal.

Leclerc carefully explained to the Naval Attaché the stability problems of the minesweepers as a class. Stability was a constant problem for the ships. After trials at Fort William it was found stability was sufficient if they carried 25 tons of ballast under the boilers and both lateral coal bunkers. However for

Addendum To Inkermann *and* Cerisoles

reasons unclear the French Naval Technical Services wanted to leave the ballast out until Montreal. Could something else be substituted? The agreed solution was as follows:

1. 16 tons of munitions (shells for the 4 inch naval guns) were spread uniformly over the bottom of the fish hold.
2. Water tanks hanging under the deck to be kept empty (4-5 tons)
3. The reserve water tanks would be kept only half full.
4. All extraneous gear stored in the fish hold (4 tons).
5. Ballast tanks kept full except for running in canals.

The arrangement proved adequate as long as they didn't steam more than two points to the wind. Closer than that and they began to founder. In simple terms the ships had to quarter into the bigger seas.

There apparently was some thought the last three ships may not be finished as the war was clearly winding down. Rather than potentially leave ammunition behind in Fort William the stock for the last three ships was divided among the proceeding six. However when it was certain the last three ships would be finished and sent off to Montreal they needed new ballast. The French substituted 30 tons of coal spread out over the bottom of the fish hold instead of the ballasting arrangements previously directed. Calculations showed the resulting stability was good and metacentric height slightly better than generally recognized as sufficient.[xiv]

It is not known whether the guns (4-inch guns fore and aft) were taken into consideration when calculating stability. They certainly had a major influence. The concern was sufficient enough the guns on earlier ships were removed in Quebec City in preparation for the Atlantic crossing. Whether this decision was the result of the *Inkermann* and *Cerisoles* loss, assuming stability was thought to be the critical problem, isn't known.

Incredibly a few days before departure from Fort William, the shipyard suggested not putting any ballast aboard the ships at all. Carpentry work in the fish hold was far behind schedule and the yard wanted to put workers aboard to complete it while the ships were underway to Montreal.[xv] Leclerc wisely refused to take responsibility for the ships if the coal ballast wasn't added to the fish hold and faced with his threat, the shipyard withdrew their request. Whether the carpentry work was done and to what standard isn't known but the ships did leave with 30 tons of coal ballast in the fish holds as required.[xvi] Regardless of the ballast issue Leclerc said he didn't like the ships. They were not sufficiently protected in the bow and not stable enough. He said he had to run for shelter in *Sebastapol* in each of lakes he crossed en route to Montreal and his successful arrival was due to luck not design. Helm

Went Missing Redux

problems continued to dog him. It failed five times, each just as he was entering a sheltered area!

He further opined, "In high, short, steep seas like on the lakes or in the ocean in the vicinity of channels, these ships will be lost if they fall broadside to the waves." He went on to say, "The ships have a smooth righting moment, slow and without lurches, so taken by broadside waves they do not have time to right themselves between two waves and rolling progressively over, they capsize by a phenomenon analogous to that of synchronous swell." There were also problems with how the coal ballast was stored since the port bunker held four to five tons more than the starboard. The water tanks for the engines were also poorly situated. Emptying one of the inboard tanks gave the ship a serious list. Clearly masters had to exercise good planning when ballasting their ships.

When Leclerc was asked by the Lieutenant what he thought happened to the *Inkermann* and *Cerisoles* he offered four theories:

1. Running Aground - It only could have happened at Manitou Island but the passage is well lit (Manitou Island Light), the night was clear and a full moon allowed land to be seen a mile off. If they went aground there a considerable amount of wreckage should have been in the area.

2. Capsizing - He felt if they went broadside to the waves, capsizing was certain. (Author's Note - As Leclerc would have realized from his experience around Manitou Island, the seas in the area can be very difficult. Dependent on wave and wind direction the seas can "bounce" off the Peninsula as well as Manitou Island, creating a very confused and dangerous sea state).

    a. An error in conning the boats could have put either or both into capsizing situation.

    b. If a servomotor (steering engine) was damaged or failed preventing the vessel from being steered or forcing her into a circle as happened to the *Sebastapol*, capsizing was almost certain. The *Sebastapol* suffered five instances of servomotor damage between Fort William and Kingston on Lake Ontario.

    c. The time required to fix the steering damage was too long. Converting the wheel to direct control took three or four minutes, an eternity if the ship is in the trough of the seas getting ready to roll. If tackle needed to be rigged between helm and rudder it could take 30 minutes to a full hour, which WAS an eternity! Could a poorly trained novice crew of "retreaded" infantry have done it?

Addendum To **Inkermann** *and* **Cerisoles**

3. Engine Damage - He largely discounted engine damage. None of the fleet on any of the delivery trips had engine problems. But he did suggest the potential for damage when the engine room was flooding. The high water sloshing back and forth could dislodge debris jamming bilge pumps or moving parts of the engine. Considering the problems the *Sebastapol* had with flooding this wasn't an unlikely scenario.
4. Collision - He only thought this possible if one ship rolled and the other came to her aid resulting in a fatal collision. But with the foul weather the captain should have been on the bridge as well as the pilot. The latter were very wary of the ships getting too close to each other regardless of the circumstance. While collision most easily explains the losses he believed it very improbable.

Leclerc finally concluded the most likely cause of loss was the result of an error at the helm. In the big seas running that night she fell off and forced into the trough, capsized. The second ship was lost the same way, either falling off herself or trying to come to the aid of her sister. It would have been a near simultaneous loss.

He thought it likely as they pulled away from the shelter of the Keweenaw they encountered bigger seas and when they saw him turn back towards land tried to follow his maneuver. He felt the chances of his capsizing during the maneuver at 50 - 50. They both came up on the short end. It would have happened between 1:00 - 3:00 am on the 24th. Had they not tried to turn but just kept running with the seas on their quarter they could have been swamped by the waves. Either way the result was the same. Had they gone too far past Manitou Island and unwilling to risk a turn back for Bete Gris, could have continued on for Grand Marais, Michigan. The Grand Marais area was smashed by a heavy blizzard and gale on the night of the 24th to the 25th, just the time the minesweepers could have arrived. When the small boat from the *Cerisoles* was found on a beach 20 miles to the east of Grand Marais it added weight to the theory. The question is how much value should be placed on the yawl? After all, she was found 90 miles from the last sighting of the *Cerisoles* and 15 days later. A lot can happen in 15 days!

Leclerc had little respect for the Great Lakes pilots, American or Canadian. None spoke French, which meant he had to station a translator aboard each ship. The quality of the translator is unknown especially when dealing with nautical terms and directions. He didn't consider the pilots, "real navigators but only experienced persons accustomed to sailing within sight of land." He also admitted complaining to them about their "extreme prudence." They were "too careful." He stated for some of them using the rules of the road meant "running" from every ship encountered. Cruising single file at close interval scared them and they often stayed too far off shore. Their only real use was in rivers, canals and in some cases, anchoring along the coasts. They were of no use running into small out of the way harbors. Their course recommendations were taken right off the charts. They were less accurate predicting weather than the French. He didn't consider them indispensable but useful only in certain situations. He claimed he wouldn't hesitate to sail without one if the need arose. Lastly he didn't like it that they had "blind faith in their compasses and log lines."[xvii]

There was also a significant problem of availability of pilots. Apparently there were difficulties during the delivery of the first ships, which caused a number of pilots to refuse to take another assignment. One in fact broke his contract after bringing the *St. Georges* down. In addition the Spanish Flu epidemic took other pilots out of the available labor pool. Canada Steamship Company had the responsibility to obtain the pilots but based on the above reasons was having an extremely difficult time in finding ones willing to take the delivery jobs![xviii]

Getting the pilots to Fort William in time for the last trip was very difficult too. The first to arrive in Fort William was delayed a day in Duluth by heavy snow, not reaching the shipyard until noon on the 22nd. The second came in on the evening train from Toronto and since Leclerc "no longer trusted him" for unknown reasons, assigned him to the *Cerisoles*. Considering Leclerc wanted to leave at midnight, the wait for pilots, especially realizing he had

The Spanish Flu killed more people than World War I and was a major public health concern for Canada.

Addendum To Inkermann *and* Cerisoles

little use for them but was required to take them, must have been galling. The last two pilots finally arrived at 11:15 a.m. on the 23rd.[xix]

French Captain Mezou of the *Cerisoles* wasn't entirely healthy. Leclerc was concerned enough about his condition he considered replacing him with Master Menard, his own second in command. Apparently this wasn't done but it does open the problem of an officer commanding one of the lost ships who wasn't physically up to the challenge.[xx]

Lieutenant De Chevigne, with the assistance of Chief Engineer Triqueneaux also took a hard look at just how the minesweepers were built at Fort William. They concluded managers ran the shipyard without an adequate background in shipbuilding. In addition the workforce was largely made up of several different nationalities lured to the yard by the high pay. Many came from the U.S. Generally speaking neither workers nor management was professionally competent. Regardless of the employee problems construction moved along rapidly with men working overtime and at night.

When a ship was declared ready by the yard and inspectors appropriate trials were held for boilers and piping, main and auxiliary engines, radios and guns. Sea trials required four hours running at full speed. Gunnery was mostly to assure the mounts were of sufficient strength to withstand the recoil. The consistent bright spot were the engines, which always ran very well.

It is worth noting while outbound from Thunder Bay Leclerc noticed his main compass, which was supposed to be compensated during trials was showing variations of 2 to 3-1/2 points between east and south. A point is 11-1/4 degrees so the variation was significant. He took a series of comparisons between his smaller steering compass and noted the difference producing an ad hoc deviation chart. It wasn't the best answer to the problem, but it gave him something to work with. If the trouble existed with his compass, it is reasonable to assume it was true for the other ships too.

While all the ships passed their sea trials the testing was always done in calm conditions. However there were still problems, which while they weren't serious enough to fail a ship, were ominous. Servomotor control shafts consistently seized up. Rivets were loose due to improper work. Leaks in the stern area were common, usually around poorly set rivet heads. The loose rivets couldn't be repaired correctly since there was no dry dock at the yard. The "fix" was simply to caulk around the rivet head. Of course in rough water when the hull worked the caulking tended to loosen allowing water to enter.

The French considered the over all workmanship to be poor, clearly the result of unskilled workforce and managers. They claimed the workers seemed to have special problems with forming the steel frames and aligning hull plates, which helped explain subsequent leaks. The work just wasn't up to French standards.[xxi] Reviewing the reports it is difficult to determine just how much of the complaining is legitimate as opposed to an attitude of French superiority. Regardless, it is fair to say the ships were roughly built with minor problems of leaking all of which could be finished up in a conventional shipyard sometime later. The lack of a dry dock at the yard can't be over emphasized. It meant once the ships were launched they stayed launched. There wasn't any opportunity to do additional hull work, easily repair rudders, shafts or propellers.

The Greatest Mystery

In my opinion the loss of the minesweepers *Inkermann* and *Cerisoles* remains the greatest mystery of Lake Superior. Perhaps the mystery is even greater than the missing *Griffon*? My viewpoint is that it certainly is far more interesting. There isn't anything unusual about a small brig disappearing with all hands in a lake gale. But two French Navy vessels going missing together with full crews, including radios and Great Lakes pilots is mind-boggling! Bear in mind though, the *Griffon*, *Inkermann* and *Cerisoles* were all French vessels!

Where the wrecks of the *Inkermann* and *Cerisoles* are is the million dollar question. Until they are found, it remains an open mystery.

My conclusion is they are either in the vicinity of Keweenaw Point as suggested by Leclerc or east of Grand Marais, Michigan on the theory the two strange ships reported by Captain Trudeau of the Grand Marais Coast Guard station were the *Inkermann* and *Cerisoles*.

Leclerc's assessment of the possibility of the two capsizing during an attempted turn or alternatively one going over and the other wrecking when attempting to rescue the crew are good theories for any location.

The loss theory for the eastern lake can't be ignored either. The Coast Guard observers were very competent and knowledgeable of all the vessels regularly in the lake and if they couldn't recognize the two strange ships close ashore the odds are they were indeed unusual ships, very possibly the missing minesweepers. Since they passed Grand Marais downbound and didn't reach the Soo, they must be lost in the eastern lake. Sinking in the eastern lake adds a modicum of credibility to the reported discovery of two skeletons in French sailor uniforms on Michipicoten Island.

I realize these locations are at best very general but without additional data, it's the best there is.

While the functional cause of loss, such as capsizing, collision or foundering due to storm stress is unknown, the moral blame can be directly assigned to the French government. For all practical purposes the war was

Addendum To Inkermann *and* Cerisoles

over on November 11, 1918. When the last three ships left Fort William it was nearly two weeks later. And the French were pushing very hard to get them from Fort William to Montreal in preparation for an Atlantic crossing. To what end? The war was over! The fact that none of the dozen would ever reach Europe shows how little needed they actually were with the conclusion of hostilities.

Consider the ships were at best marginally fitted out from the yard. Remember the non-compensated compasses as an example. The crews were not trained sailors by any stretch of the imagination. Even if they were all veterans of Columbus' first voyage, time was needed to shakedown the new boats, to work out the problems of the craft and give the crew a chance to learn the ship. Instead it was go, go, go! Plus they were sailing into the Great Lakes in the deep fall, so far into the storm season many big steamers already were laid up for winter. That the last three were hammered by a storm on Lake Superior was only to be expected. Leclerc's failure to work with his Great Lakes pilots certainly contributed to the whole debacle.

Every once in a while a story bubbles up that one or both of the missing minesweepers was located but the finder of course is keeping quiet about it. I doubt such tales have any truth to them. It is important to realize that when they are found, and certainly they will be, the French government will have great legal interest in them. After all they still own the pair. They remain French Navy vessels and considering the extreme loss of French officers and men, will certainly be considered a gravesite.

TOO SMALL TO DO THE JOB - THE *LAMBTON*

From the very earliest days of Great Lakes shipping establishing and maintaining aids to navigation (lighthouses to most people), has been critical. Today lighthouse "junkies" argue the pros and cons of the various lights, eagerly have their "passports" stamped for each one they visit and happily snap away with their cameras "documenting" every beacon found.

As a maritime historian I find it fascinating they dote on the history of the dead stone towers rather than focus on the more exciting heritage of America's first heroes, the men of the old U.S. Life-Saving Service and to a point, early Coast Guard. It seems the "lighthouse mafia" has convinced a generation of Americans that somehow the lighthouses were something more than just glorified illuminated and very expensive coastal highway signs! The real stories are the old life-savers, the iron-willed men who lived their motto, "Regulations say we have to go out. They don't say anything about coming back." The lighthouse motto of "We'll leave a light on for you" pales in comparison.[i] But I digress.

It is sill argued on Lake Superior which light is the oldest. Both Copper Harbor on the Keweenaw Peninsula and Whitefish Point to the east were established in 1849 and since the records are confused enough it isn't possible to determine which was actually illuminated first. While which was first may be puzzling the newest one isn't. The records show the last major light established on the lake was at Sand Hills on the west side of the Keweenaw in 1919.

Of course many other lights were built on Superior between 1849 and 1919. An entire federal system was created to design, build, operate and maintain American lights on the Great Lakes as well as saltwater coasts.

The Sand Hills Light was the last built on Lake Superior. Author

Critical to the operation was the unglamorous lighthouse tender. On the American side of the lakes boats like the *Marigold* and *Hollyhock* delivered keepers, crews and supplies to the isolated stations in the spring and returned for them in the fall when navigation closed. For many years the Canadians didn't provide this basic service to Great Lakes lightkeepers expecting them to reach isolated stations on their own in the spring and get home the same way in the fall. Invariably this meant using a small sailboat since none of the men were well off enough to engage a proper and safe boat. (if they had that kind of money they wouldn't be lightkeepers). Only after several keepers lost their lives attempting to handle the travel themselves did the Canadian government recognize it as an essential service and task lighthouse tenders with the job.[ii] However unlike the American tenders, purposely designed, built, equipped and manned for the job, the Canadians often skimped by using chartered tugs or tenders not constructed or well planned for the specialized tasks required. This was especially true in the early days of the nation. Generally this ad hoc system worked but not always. Some of the

Too Small To Do The Job - The Lambton

ships were unsafe and never should have been on the lakes; and therein is the story of the *Lambton*.

Shipwreck buffs are well familiar with the tales of the long lost *Bannockburn*, *Henry B. Smith* and *D. M. Clemson* but the little *Lambton* often draws a blank.

The *Lambton* was built in the Canadian government shipyard at Sorel in 1909. Twin engined and twin screwed, she also had passenger cabins on the main deck to accommodate several lightkeepers and their families. At 108-feet overall, 25 feet in beam and 13-feet in depth, she was a very small boat to brave Superior's gales but over the years somehow managed to survive without major incident. However some marine men thought she was running on borrowed time. She couldn't cheat the lake forever.

Technically she was classed as a "lighthouse supply and buoy vessel," and performed this service regularly being responsible for the area from Quebec north to the Upper Lakes, including Georgian Bay, Lakes Huron and Superior and sometimes Lake Erie too. It was a massive operational area and far too large for such a small boat. Not only did she deliver people, food, fuel and all manner of supplies but she also serviced and replaced all buoys and related navigation aids as needed. Again, it was far too much for such a small boat and crew to do. Regardless of her modest size and overwhelming workload, her crews took pride it her. Her white hull and decks were kept spotless, often scrubbed with "soogee," a mixture of lye and soap boiled together with a steam pipe. If it didn't take the dirt off the ship, it did take skin off the sailors hands applying it!

The tug Lambton *on the launching ways. Author*

The Lambton *and the* Simcoe. *Both would be lost to shipwreck.* Ministry of Transport

The *Lambton* was based at the Parry Sound agency of the Department of Marine and Fisheries with her larger running mate *Simcoe*.

The 180-foot *Simcoe* was also a victim of shipwreck. On Saturday, December 7, 1917 she foundered with all hands in a storm southwest of the Magdalen Islands in the Gulf of St. Lawrence. She was en route from the Upper Lakes to the Bay of Fundy to relieve the *C.G.S. Dollard* when the disaster occurred. The loss has never been fully explained.[iii]

The *Lambton* left the Canadian Soo at 10:30 a.m. Tuesday, April 18, 1922 in company of the big steel Playfair steamers *Glenlivet* and *Glenfinnan*.

Too Small To Do The Job - The Lambton

The steamer Glenfinnan *was one of the last ships to see the* Lambton *afloat. Hamilton Collection*

The *Lambton's* job was to place the lights in service at Ile Parisienne on the north side of Whitefish Bay and at Caribou and Michipicoten Islands. To this end she carried all the keepers and their supplies. A total of 22 men were aboard the small tug including the crew. All the lights were important aids for Lake Superior shipping, although perhaps more so for the Canadian traffic running to and from Port Arthur-Fort William and the Soo.

At the time she reached Whitefish Point heavy northwest gales were sweeping down the lake and snow squalls were reported in some locations. More ominously the wind packed drifting ice into Whitefish Bay. It had previously been ice-free.

At 8:30 p.m. on April 19th the Soo was hammered by a powerful windstorm out of the northwest. Since the *Lambton* was known to be on the lake, many folks privately expressed concern for her safety. Inquiries were made on the 20th and 21st for her status and whereabouts but all came back negative. No one had seen or heard anything of her.

Finally on the evening of the 21st the radio operator at the Soo reported the *Glenfinnan* reported she last saw the, "*Lambton* at 2:00 p.m. on the 19th, 40 miles out from Whitefish Point heading for Caribou Island." The following day the *Glenfinnan* radioed the Caribou light was still not burning, a bad omen for the fate of the *Lambton*.

On the 23rd the downbound Canadian steamer *Valcartier* radioed the Canadian Marine agent at the Soo she had seen nothing of the missing *Lambton* but at 6:30 a.m. on the 20th "about 25 miles southeast of

WENT MISSING REDUX

Lonely Caribou Island Light was an important aid for Canadian shipping. Author

Michipicoten Island and 15 miles east of Caribou, saw what looked like the top of a small pilothouse painted white, trimmed with bright red," and some additional wreckage. Since the wheelsman on the *Valcartier* sailed the year prior on the *Lambton* he was certain it was hers. The area of sighting was only slightly off the normal vessel track.

The Canadian government took no action concerning the missing *Lambton* until the evening of the 23rd when the Superintendent of Lights Mr. J.N. Arthurs, returned to his residence after delivering the lightkeepers at Griffith Island, Richards Landing and Shoal Island on the Canadian side of the lower St. Marys River. Arthurs knew nothing about the missing *Lambton* until he arrived home. Regardless of the lackadaisical attitude of the government to this point Arthurs jumped right in to straighten out the mess. He immediately contacted the Canadian authorities to authorize a full search and arranged for the charter of the Lake Superior Paper Company tug *G. R. Gray*. She was the only suitable vessel already fitted out for the season and ready to go. It is amazing no other Canadian government official apparently made the least effort to start a search or notify higher-ups of the *Lambton* problem. It was almost like the attitude was, "lets wait for Arthurs to get back. He can take care of it."

He quickly arranged for substitute lightkeepers and additional supplies and loaded everything and everybody aboard the *Gray*. By 6:30 p.m. the following day they were out bound from the Soo. Hitting heavy pack ice in lower Whitefish Bay she was forced to anchor off Point au Pins and wait for an upbound freighter to break a path. At 10:00 a.m. on the 25th one passed and the tug was duly following in her wake to open water.

Too Small To Do The Job - The **Lambton**

Steamers trapped in Lake Superior ice. If the ice was thick enough and winds contrary, there was a real danger of running out of fuel and food. Author

Passing Ile Parisienne Island he noted neither light nor foghorn was operating. Since the ice was too thick to make a landing on the island to investigate he and his men continued on to Whitefish Point where the government wireless station operator told him the Parisienne Light hadn't been seen yet this season. Arthur surmised the ice had been too thick for the *Lambton* to land also so she must have continued on, likely for Michipicoten Island.

During the next five days the tug thoroughly searched eastern Lake Superior; not only looking at and around Caribou and Michipicoten Islands, but also coasting the entire shore from the Michipicoten River south to Whitefish Bay and methodically cruising the open lake. The U.S. Coast Guard Cutter *Cook* assisted by coasting the American south shore. The *Cook* was successful in finding wreckage. Pushing through ice fields she located part of a cabin with white woodwork, a door, a bracket lamp with a nickel-plated matchbox and other material. Canadian sailors familiar with the *Lambton* readily identified it as hers.[iv]

Arthurs also alerted all area lightkeepers to keep a sharp eye for wreckage and made persistent inquiries of commercial freighters. Someone had to have information on the missing tug!

To gain a fuller appreciation of the search effort eventually made for the *Lambton* this writer carefully plotted the movement of the *Gray* and those of assisting vessels and made the proper time notations for each. In examining the results two facts become evident. First the *Gray* made a painstaking search

WENT MISSING REDUX

The 110-foot Coast Guard Cutter Cook *was a former World War I Navy submarine chaser. For a time she was stationed at Grand Marais, Michigan. The Coast Guard had several of the class but they proved too expensive to maintain and operate. The* Cook *was sold surplus in 1936 but saw service again in World War II when a dearth of small coastal patrol craft was filled by almost anything that could float including private yachts. Author*

and second Arthurs and the tug were constantly on the move. It seems doubtful that Arthurs was able at anytime to snatch more than an hour's quick nap.

Meanwhile more clues to the *Lambton's* last trip trickled in to authorities. On April 23 the *Glenlivet* reported sighting the *Lambton* on the 19th, 40 miles above Whitefish Point. Her steering gear was disabled and she was steering with jury-rigged cables. The steamer *Osler* also reported seeing her on the 19th at approximately the same location and that the height of the gale struck about two hours afterward. The *Osler* made no mention of a steering problem nor did the steamer *Westmount* who also saw the tug about the same time and location.

The most ominous report came from the steamer *Midland Prince*. She said around noon on the 19th she saw the *Lambton* but lost track of her in the gale. During the height of the storm which was short and vicious, the wind swinging from southeast to northeast and quickly increasing to become one of the worst blows the ship's officers could remember. When the gale passed the *Lambton* was out of sight.

More and more stories of the last trip of the *Lambton* continued to filter in to the Soo. It seems that while the *Glenfinnan*, *Glenlivet* and *Lambton* were working their way through Whitefish Bay the *Glenfinnan* stalled in the ice field. The smaller and more nimble *Lambton* managed to break the big steamer free. The tug didn't have the power to just smash the ice as a real ice-

Too Small To Do The Job - The Lambton

The Midland Prince *was one of the last ships to see the* Lambton *afloat.*
Hamilton Collection

breaker would have, but by carefully ramming at the edges of the ice, backing and ramming again, she was able to "nibble" at the ice and free the *Glenfinnan*. However in her maneuvering she collided with the steamer with her port quarter. The *Glenfinnan's* captain said neither vessel was damaged. However he also stated before the three ships cleared the ice field the *Lambton* broke her steering gear and rigged one-inch hawsers to her quadrant <u>without</u> using tackle.[v] The quadrant is a 90 degree steel yoke used to control the rudder.

The *Lambton* had a Drake Steam Steering Engine in the pilothouse and the (rudder and quadrant) cables were connected to it. To use the steering engine the wheel only had to be turned enough to open a valve and the steam gear would run until shut off. With the valve activated the drum with the chain (much like an anchor windlass) moved the rudder the required amount. Think of it as the same concept as a car's power steering. In theory the power of the steering engine was sufficient to move the quadrant and rudder. Consider the similarities with the minesweeper's "servomotor" described in the *Inkermann* and *Cerisoles* story. Regardless of the steering engine, because she had twin screws and two engines, it was more difficult for a wheelsman to effectively control in the best of conditions not considering storm or ice. Partially this

WENT MISSING REDUX

The Lambton *with full "holiday" pendants flying. Author*

was because unlike modern ships, the engines were controlled in the engine room. The captain relayed engine commands to the engineer by a "Chadburn" or engine room telegraph, a mechanical device with a dial and two indicators. A similar device is in the engineroom. The dial is divided into different speeds, which are sent below by moving the indicator. The engineer makes the necessary engine adjustments and sets his indicator on the same speed, which is relayed to the pilothouse confirming his engine setting. Since there were two engines there were two "Chadburns."

The fact the *Lambton* had to rig hawsers (cables), in effect emergency steering, indicates she suffered steering damage in the ice, a not uncommon occurrence for a vessel working ice with an unprotected rudder.[vi] By contrast U.S. Lighthouse tenders intended for northern waters were designed to work in ice from their very inception.

The steering arrangement on the *Lambton* was especially subject to ice damage. She was built as a tug and rode comparatively low in the water exposing the steering quadrant and cable to freezing spray. It wasn't uncommon for crewmen to have to chop ice off the cable and quadrant, a dangerous situation reflecting the poor design.

Should the steering engine fail, it was necessary to rig a complete tackle system in place of it. Apparently she just rigged temporary hawsers (cables), not tackle, a system of blocks and lines, to control the rudder. Without the

Too Small To Do The Job - The **Lambton**

mechanical advantage of tackle, it would be far more difficult to steer the ship, especially in heavy sea conditions. Perhaps adequate tackle wasn't aboard. If so, the *Lambton* was remarkably poorly equipped and should have immediately returned to the Soo for repair immediately on sustaining damage. Continuing on with such a jury-rigged steering system was foolish.

The *Lambton's* lifeboats were also kept on the upper deck, a location making it very difficult for the crew to reach them in a storm. When one of the boats was eventually found drifting between Caribou and Michipicoten Islands after the wreck it's internal air tanks were crushed, evidence the lifeboat sank with the ship before finally breaking free, the water pressure crushing her tanks.

It is important to understand the very job of lighthouse tenders is to go in harms way. After all lighthouses and buoys are intended to warn ships away from hazards. To service the various aids to navigation tenders have to go very close to the hazard and be prepared to suffer (and survive) potential damage. Often it is necessary to put a bow in the weeds ashore to allow the tender to reach a difficult aid, work in strong current or other hazardous conditions. Running in early or late season ice and stormy weather isn't unusual. The shame was the *Lambton* wasn't a bigger and stronger vessel for the job she was given.

The three boats, *Lambton*, *Glenfinnan* and *Glenlivet*, remained together until 2:00 p.m. when they were roughly 35 miles above Whitefish Point. At this point the weather began to deteriorate and the two big Playfair steamers wisely returned to the shelter of Whitefish Point, arriving barely ten minutes before the full fury of the gale struck. The *Lambton* however didn't run for shelter but continued on westward.

The weather logs for the eastern lake all agree that on April 19th a northeast gale began approximately 2:00 p.m. peaking around 6:00 p.m. when the station at Whitefish Point recorded a wind speed of 69 miles per hour. Doubtless there were local variations and faster speeds out on the lake.

Additional *Lambton* wreckage was found by the steamer *Grant Morden* 14 miles northwest of Crisp's Point, a dozen miles to the west of Whitefish Point. The steamer *Collingwood* later ran through the same wreckage field.

After going over all the facts, Superintendent Arthurs concluded the *Lambton* foundered about 6:00 p.m. on the 19th, somewhere on a track between Caribou Island and Gargantua. He believed when the gale struck, the *Lambton* was running for shelter on the north shore since the wind was blowing northeast. She just ran out of time to reach shelter.

The *Lambton* was only 13 years old and a reasonably seaworthy vessel within the limits of her design. Having weathered other gales why did she succumb to this one. My conclusion is she foundered as a direct result of her

WENT MISSING REDUX

jury-rigged and inadequate steering gear. With only direct ropes and no tackle rigged to multiply the effort of the men, she was a doomed boat when the waves ran high.

If the *Lambton* fell into the trough of the waves it would have been nearly impossible to extricate herself. Wallowing in the trough she rolled onto her beam ends and dropped for the bottom.

Through the bright illumination of hindsight we can conclude the master of the *Lambton* made a series of horrible decisions. He should have rigged the more efficient tackle for his rudder quadrant when first damaged in the ice. After making emergency repairs he compounded his error by not returning immediately to the Soo for proper and complete repair. Even after he continued on with the Playfair boats he should have returned with them to Whitefish Point for shelter rather than continuing on alone when the storm threatened. Should he have encountered additional problems running back with them, he had help at hand, something he didn't when he continued alone.

Other than that mentioned, no other wreckage of the *Lambton* has ever been found, or has a single body of a crewman or lightkeeper been discovered. It can only be concluded they were all trapped in the hull when she headed for the bottom.

Certainly the Canadian government was at fault for committing such a poor excuse for ship to perform the demanding duty of a lighthouse tender on Lake Superior. It was a policy that placed the lives of all who sailed aboard her, crew, keepers or families, at grave risk.

The Lambton *being overwhelmed by a Lake Superior gale. By the late maritime illustrator Edward Pusick.* Author

Too Small To Do The Job - The Lambton

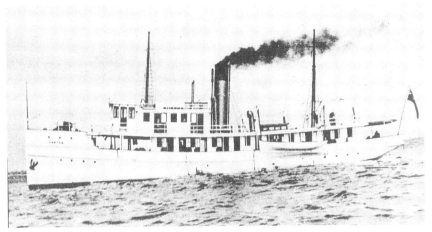

The Lambton *was a small ship to face Superior's gales. Author*

One keeper was immensely fortunate in the *Lambton* debacle. Perhaps he had a premonition or just didn't like the ship. Regardless of why Michipicoten Island keeper Charles Miron literally "missed the boat" and instead journeyed to his station via the Algoma Central Railroad to a point opposite the island, hiked four miles through the woods to a lumber camp and used their small launch to run the 15 miles to the island where he again hiked to his lighthouse. It was a round about way to travel, but at least he arrived alive. Since he was originally thought to be on the lost *Lambton* it took some time to sort out that he was alive with relatives and various bureaucrats.[vii]

How Caribou Island keeper George Penefold came to be aboard the *Lambton* is another tale. The previous keeper quit Caribou because the government refused to provide safe transportation to or from the island. Caribou Island was a good 35 miles out in the lake to the west of Cape Gargantua, a long run in good weather and an murderous one in foul. The original light was established in 1886 and rebuilt into a 125-foot high flying buttress tower in 1912.

Since the keeper had a large family and the pay wasn't sufficient for him to buy life insurance and of course the parsimonious Canadian government would not provide even a minimal "death gratuity" in the event he was lost at sea, he quit the job. George Penefold took his place but his wife was well aware of the dangers of going it alone from Caribou Island. She started a letter writing campaign to convince the government lighthouse bureaucrats to at least transport the keepers to and from the isolated lights.

Doubtless the December 1916 experience of the Michipicoten Island keeper and his son were deeply implanted in her mind. Michipicoten Island was 20 miles to the north of Caribou and an easier place to travel to and from. The two men left the island on the 16th in their 18-foot boat bound for Gargantua on the mainland, 20-odd miles to the east. They delayed leaving as long as possible but finally had a break in the weather and knew if they didn't leave then they would never have a better chance. About 14 miles out a northeaster slammed hard into them. The lightkeeper later related, "Our pump froze and we had to take to the oars. It was 12 degrees below zero at Gargantua that night. Our boat began to take in water and we gradually had to throw everything we had away to keep afloat. First we threw away 25 gallons of oil, then an emergency sail we were carrying and finally our provisions. Our bodies were caked in ice and we could hardly bend either our legs or arms. One of the oars slipped away from my son in the afternoon and he reached for it but slipped over the side of the boat; but fortunately I grabbed him and got him out of the water."

Driven by wind and wave the pair finally fetched up on Leach Island, several miles off the mainland. They stayed for three days living only on a few biscuits and warming by a bonfire they managed to spark to life.

The keeper went on, "The boat was in pretty bad condition, but I fixed it up as well as I could… we struck out for the North Shore which was three miles distant, my son at the oars and I bailing all the way. There was not much of a sea on but it was bitterly cold and the wind was quite high. We finally struck the North Shore after five hours between Gargantua and Telegram Rock. There was a hill a short distance away and my son crawled to it, from which point he could see the islands lying off Gargantua. All the time we were carrying with us a puppy, which we had brought up in the spring. We killed him when we struck the North Shore and this kept us alive until we struck Gargantua. We could only travel very slowly and we had to crawl most of the way. Between us and Gargantua there were a number of bluffs and we had to go around most of these… we finally arrived on the 22nd." Both men were badly frozen around the hands and feet, but eventually recovered.[viii]

The small minded men in Ottawa had little understanding of difficulty of keeping a light on Superior, especially just getting to and from it without government assistance but the campaign succeeded thus George Penefold was aboard the *Lambton* when she left the dock in the Soo. The road to hell is truly paved with good intentions.

END NOTES

Captain Napier's Last Trip - The Alpena

[i]*Holland City News*, November 6, 1880.

[ii]Shipwrecks - http://www.boatnerd.com; The Loss of the *Sultana* - http://www.navyandmarine.org/ondeck/1862sultana.htm

[iii]Dwight Boyer, *Ghost Ships of the Great Lakes*,(New York: Dodd, Mead and Company, 1968), p. 182.

[iv]James L. Elliott, *Red Stacks Over the Horizon* (Grand Rapids: William B. Eerdmanns Publishing Company, 1967), p. 71.

[v]*Chicago Daily Tribune*, October 20, 1880.

[vi]At that price it is worth speculating whether an enterprising citizen went into the business of "marking" life jackets! Such things have been done before.

[vii]*Chicago Daily Tribune*, October 20, 1880

[viii]Shipwrecks - http://www.boatnerd.com.

[ix]*Saugatuck Tribune*, October 29, 1880.

[x]The *Waubuno* was a Canadian propeller lost on November 22, 1879 with all hands on Georgian Bay. Reportedly the wife of one of the passengers, Dr. Dupe, had premonition of disaster and begged her husband to cancel the trip. He didn't and they sailed off into oblivion.

[xi]*Holland City News*, October 30, 1880.

[xii]*Red Stacks*, p. 59.

[xiii]*Holland City News*, November 6, 1880.

[xiv] *Muskegon Daily Chronicle*, October 25, 1880.

[xv] Elizabeth Sherman, *Beyond the Windswept Dunes, the Story of Maritime Muskegon*, (Detroit: Wayne State University Press, 2003), p. 73.

[xvi] AKA North Point Light.

[xvii] *Chicago Daily Tribune*, October 19, 1880.

[xviii] *Lady Elgin* - www.boatnerd.com.

Lost Off The Keweenaw, the Manistee

[i] During this period of history under ordinary circumstances the useful life of a wooden vessel was considered about 15 years. After 25 years they were usually thought too far gone to be of value. (Inch, *Great Lakes Wooden Shipbuilding Era*.)

[ii] Some sources report the Manitowoc rebuild as occurring in 1881.

[iii] She would have reached Portage via the Portage Lake Ship Canal finished in 1874. The canal cut through the Keweenaw Peninsula allowing ships to avoid the long and treacherous trip around Keweenaw Point.

[iv] There is some discussion concerning the actual date of the *Manistee's* departure. I elected to use the date as reported in the November 22, 1883, *Portage Lake Mining Gazette*.

[v] A "Texas" was the structure immediately behind the upper deck of a steamer, usually containing the officer's cabins, etc. The pilothouse was in front or on top; *Portage Lake Mining Gazette*, November 22, 1883.

[vi] *Daily Mining Gazette*, November 22, 1883.

[vii] *Ashland Daily Press*, May 17, 1883.

[viii] Journal of the Light Station at Eagle Harbor, November 1883.

[ix] *Portage Lake Mining Gazette*, June 19, 1884.

[x] *Marquette Mining Journal*, November 24, 1883.

[xi] The wooden steamer SUNBEAM was forced on her beam ends during a gale on August 28, 1863 while somewhere off Eagle River. Only one of her 35 passengers and crew survived the wreck.

[xii] *Mining Journal*, December 27, 1883.

End Notes

xiii*Ashland Press*, December 25, 1883.

xiv Superior Shoal is located roughly in mid-lake. See the *Bannockburn* chapter for more details.

xv Ivan Walton Collection, Box 6, Bentley Historical Library, University of Michigan.

xvi*Portage Lake Mining Gazette*, December 6, 1883.

Questions, Always Questions - The W.H. Gilcher

i *Annual Report, Lake Carriers Association 1910.*

ii The *Spokane* was lengthened by 60 feet in 1892 at the Cleveland Ship Building Company.

iii*Marine Review*, February 28, 1892.

iv Richard Wright, *Freshwater Whales*, Kent State University Press, 1969, p. 43.

v Western Reserve Sinks - http://query.nytimes.com/gst/abstract.html?res=9503E2D8173BEE33A25751C0A96F9C94639ED7CF; *History of the Great Lakes*, Philip J. Minch - http://www.halinet.on.ca/GreatLakes/Documents/HGL2/default.asp?ID=s834.

vi*Marine Review*, December 25, 1892.

vii*Marine Review*, September 12, 1892.

viii*Onoko* - http://www.mnhs.org/places/nationalregister/shipwrecks/onoko/onocac.html.

ix Wright, Richard J. *A History of the American Ship Building Company and its Predecessors*. Kent State University Press, 1969, p. 37.

x*Leelanau Enterprise*, June 12, 2007.

xi Philip J. Minch - http://www.linkstothepast.com/marine/captainsMi.html#minchphilipj.

xii 1949 Armistice Day Storm - http://www.boatnerd.com/news/archive/11-98.htm.

xiii Cleveland History - http://ech.case.edu/ech-cgi/article.pl?id=ASBC.

WENT MISSING REDUX

[xiv] The number of crew varies with the source. I am using the number developed by David Swazye as hosted on Boatnerd.com.

[xv] Daily Log, U.S. Life-Saving Station at North Manitou Island, October 28-31, 1892.

[xvi] Some sources identify the captain as "Lloyd" Weeks.

[xvii] Marine History of the Great Lakes, http://www.hhpl.on.ca/GreatLakes/Wrecks/details.asp?ID=22456; Leeds H. Weeks was born in Brownhelm, Lorain Co., Ohio, in 1843, son of Lawrence D. Weeks, a pioneer shipbuilder and owner. Captain Weeks commenced sailing at an early age and when he was twenty-one was in command of the schooner *Idaho*, which was owned by his father. Subsequently he sailed as mate and seaman in a number of vessels, being the master of the scow *H.H. Hines*, engaged in the lumber trade between Alpena and Cleveland, in 1880. During the next three seasons he was master of the schooners *C.P. Minch*, *W.S. Crosthwaite*, *Crosby*, and *B.F. Bruce*, respectively. During the winter of 1883 he rebuilt the *Oregon* in Buffalo, sailing her for two months of the next season. He sailed the *Horace B. Tuttle* for a time that year, and then went to Trenton, Michigan, to oversee the building of the steamer *J.C. Gilchrist*. Captain Weeks was in employ of the *Gilchrist* for many years, being commodore, captain, and in charge of all the building and extensive repairs. After the *J.C. Gilchrist* was completed, he took her out new and sailed her until the close of that season, 1890. In 1891, Captain Weeks brought out the new steamer *W.H. Gilcher*, sailed her all that season and until October 12, 1892, when she was lost with all hands in a storm on Lake Michigan. During his long and active connection with the lake marine, Captain Weeks became interested in a number of vessels. At the time of his death he owned shares in the *Gilcher*, *Craig*, *Minch*, *Bruce*, *Oregon* and *Hiawatha*. In 1868, he was married to Miss Gertrude Lyman, of Sandusky, who was born in Germany and removed to the United States at the age of ten years. Their children were Hattie, who died at the age of five years; Sarah, now Mrs. W.E. Beely, of Vermilion; and Lawrence D., who is chief engineer of the steamer *J.C. Lockwood*. (previous from Mansfield - History of the Great Lakes, Volume II).

[xviii] Strongbacks were supports for canvas lifeboat covers.

[xix] Daily Log, North Manitou Island Life-Saving Station, October - November 1892. NARA; *Detroit Free Press*, November 5, 1902.

End Notes

[xx]Pitz, Herbert. *Lake Michigan Disasters*. Manitowoc, 1925, p. 54.

[xxi]*Detroit Free Press*, November 5, 1892.

[xxii]*Leelanau Enterprise*, January 5, 1893.

[xxiii]*Chicago Inter-Ocean*, November 2, 1892.

[xxiv]Wright, *Whales*, p. 36.

[xxv]Frank Blair was involved in a number of salvage operations. For example in October 1919 the steamer *Frank O'Connor* burned and sank in 60-feet of water off Cana Island at the north end of the Door Peninsula. Blair teamed with Charles Innes to recover 100 tons of the coal. As a Chicago diver he performed a number of crime related services. For example he recovered the typewriter used to help convict the notorious murderers Leopold and Loeb from the Jackson Park Lagoon in 1924. In August 1929 he recovered counterfeit seals for the University of Chicago and Northwestern University. They were vital evidence in convicting a ring of eight men, including the head of the Illinois Department of Registration and Education for selling forged medical degrees, *Time Magazine*, August 19, 1929.

Lost Off The Keweenaw, The Hudson

[i]The statement "cleared Eagle River" is interesting. The U.S. Life-Saving Service official report of loss indicates she was downbound from Duluth and makes no mention of Eagle River. The term "cleared" as used by Miss Bennett must have meant passed as in "passed Eagle River."

[ii]He was also reported as being her wheelsman.

[iii]*Daily Mining Gazette*, September 21, 1901.

[iv]*Daily Mining Gazette*, September 21, 1901.

[v]*Daily Mining Gazette*, September 27, 1901.

[vi]*Daily Mining Gazette*, October 8, 1901.

[vii]*Daily Mining Gazette*, October 1, 1901.

[viii]*Daily Mining Journal*, November 12, 1901.

[ix]*Daily Mining Journal*, September 23, 1901.

[x]*Annual Report, U.S. Steamboat Inspection Service 1902*, p. 77.

[xi]*Daily Mining Journal*, October 8, 1901.

[xii]*Daily Mining Gazette*, September 28, 1901.

[xiii]*Daily Mining Journal*, October 9, 1901.

[xiv]McLean only saw her in a "sinking condition." The keeper's daughter and others who later claimed to have seen her only did so through the curtain of a heavy gale at a distance of several miles, not good conditions for detailed observation. Strangely there is no entry in the lighthouse log concerning the *Hudson*.

[xv]*Daily Mining Gazette*, September 21, 1901.

[xvi]*Tioga* - Stonehouse Collection; *Tioga* - http://www.boatnerd.com.

[xvii]Runge Collection, Wisconsin Marine Historical Society.

[xviii]Beacons in the Night, Clarke Historical Library - http://clarke.cmich.edu/lighthouses/lhkeep1.htm.

[xix]Stonehouse, Frederick. *Isle Royale Shipwrecks*, Gwinn, Michigan: Avery Color Studios, 1992, pp. 43-49.

[xx]George C. Mason, "A Partial Listing of the Hull Numbers of Ships Built by the Component Shipyards of the American Shipbuilding Company, Cleveland, Ohio." *Inland Seas*, Winter, 1952.

[xxi]*Daily Mining Gazette*, September 23, 1901.

[xxii]*Hudson* - www.boatnerd.com/shipwrecks/.

[xxiii]Joseph M. Overfield. *The Last Voyage of the* Hudson. (Kenmore, NY: Ken-Ton Printing Company, 1981), p. 1.

[xxiv]*Daily Mining Gazette*, September 23, 1901.

[xxv]*Evening News* (Saulte St. Marie, Michigan), November 5, 1904.

[xxvi]Frederick Stonehouse, *Haunted Lakes, Great Lakes Ghost Stories, Superstitions and Sea Serpents*, Duluth: Lake Superior Port Cities, 1997), pp. 85-88.

A Victim Of Superior Shoal? - Bannockburn

[i]A second sighting by another vessel placed her 30 miles off Keweenaw Point and 40 miles from Isle Royale. The difference between the two locations is comparatively small.

End Notes

[ii]*Duluth News-Tribune*, November 29, 1902.

[iii]*U.S. Lake Survey, Survey of the Northern and Northwestern Lakes, Great Lakes Pilot 1955*, p. 83.

[iv]John F. Devendorf, *Great Lakes Bulk Carriers 1869-1985* (Niles, Michigan: John F. Davendorf); 1995, p. 68.; Rev. Peter Van Der Linden, Ed., *Great Lakes Ships We Remember* (Cleveland, Ohio: Marine Historical Society of Detroit), 1979, p. 219.

[v]There is a fundamental difference between "grounding" and "stranding." The term grounding means running on an underwater part of a reef or shoal, while stranding refers to running on to dry land. The Sand Beach incident was reported as a stranding although I suspect it was really a grounding. The potential for damaging the ship is the same.

[vi]Stanley Fillmore and R.W. Sandilands. *The Chartmakers, the History of Nautical Surveying in Canada.* (NC Press Limited), 1983, p. 161 - 162, 165.

[vii]BAYFIELD - http://www.canfoh.org/Ships/Bayfield.htm#II.

[viii]Passage Island is the turn point for ships going to and from the Canadian Lakehead, previously ports called Port Arthur and Fort William but today known as Thunder Bay.

[ix]Frederick Stonehouse. *Went Missing.* (Gwinn, Michigan: Avery Color Studios, 1984), pp. 137-140; BAYFIELD - http://www.canfoh.org/Ships/Bayfield.htm#II.

"Freshwater, Bah!" - The **Adella Shores**

[i]"Schooner-Barges" were old schooners with cut down rigs, usually the topmasts removed. Donkey steam engines were added for deck power and crews reduced to perhaps three to four men instead of seven or eight if fully rigged.

[ii]Ship Naming, http://en.wikipedia.org/wiki/Ship_naming_and_launching.

[iii]The *Mackinaw II*, known too as the *"Mini Mac"* because of her smaller size, 240 feet as compared to the original *Mackinaw's* 291 feet. The original *Mackinaw* was an ice breaker, a mission she performed extraordinarily well. The *Mini Mac* is multipurpose, in theory not only breaking ice but servicing buoys, recovering pollution, Search and Rescue,

etc., kind of a "Swiss Army knife" of the lakes. And many folks fear like a Swiss Army knife while it may be capable of doing many things, it will do none of them well. Only time will tell and at this writing the jury is still very much out.

[iv] *Duluth News Tribune*, May 9, 1909.

[v] *Duluth News Tribune*, May 10, 1909.

[vi] *Nor'Easter*, Journal of the Lake Superior Marine Museum Association, Volume 21, Number 1, January-February 1996, p. 3.

[vii] *Duluth News Tribune*, December 2, 1901.

[viii] *Evening News*, May 8, 1909.

[ix] *Evening News*, May 7, 1909.

[x] *Daily Mining Journal*, May 10, 1909.

[xi] Daily Log, U.S. Life-Saving Station Grand Marais, Michigan, May 1909

[xii] *Duluth News Tribune*, May 11, 1909.

[xiii] *Duluth Herald*, May 8, 1909.

[xiv] Some sources identify him as "Siebert."

[xv] *Telescope*, January-February 1993, p. 10.

[xvi] *Aurania* File, Stonehouse Collection.

[xvii] *George Nester* - http://www.boatnerd.com/

"Bucking Into The Teeth Of The Gale - The Henry B. Smith*

[i] Beeson, Harvey C., *Beesons' Inland Marine Directory*, 1913.

[ii] In old charts Ile Parisienne was called Parisian Island.

[iii] *Daily Mining Journal*, November 15, 1913.

[iv] *Annual Report, U.S. Life-Saving Service*, 1913.

[v] *Ludington Daily News*, November 3, 1983; E-mail, Paul W. Schopp to author, June 8, 1997.

[vi] Newspaper Clipping, unidentified, undated.

End Notes

[vii] John O Greenwood. *The Fleet Histories, Volume Six* (Cleveland: Freshwater Press, 1998), p. 147

[viii] John O Greenwood. *The Fleet Histories, Volume Six* (Cleveland: Freshwater Press, 1998), p147-153.

[ix] Logbook, U.S. Life-Saving Station at Marquette, Michigan November 9, 1913.

[x] *Daily Mining Journal*, November 13, 1913.

[xi] *Daily Mining Journal*, November 13, 1913.

[xii] *Daily Mining Journal*, November 16, 1913.

[xiii] *Daily Mining Journal*, November 20, 1913.

[xiv] *Daily Mining Journal*, November 20, 1913.

[xv] *Daily Mining Journal*, November 24, 1913.

[xvi] *Daily Mining Journal*, November 16, 1913.

[xvii] Steamship *J.B. Ford* - http://www.steamshipjbfordhistoricalsurvey.com/.

[xviii] *Evening News* (Sault Ste. Marine, Michigan), November 22, 1913.

[xix] *Daily Mining Journal*, November 15, 1913.

[xx] *Daily Mining Journal*, November 15, 1913.

[xix] *Daily Mining Journal*, November 16, 1913.

[xxii] Rattray was accurately forecasting the future of lifeboats but not on the Great Lakes. For the last 30 years plus saltwater ships have been using a survival capsule type of lifeboat as a way of abandoning ship. Kept ready on set of rails at the stern of a ship, the crew only has to climb, seal it up and internally release the boat to self launch. Lakers still use lifeboats on davits, the best technology of the last century although self-inflating life rafts are also carried. Getting into either in the midst of a storm is very difficult.

[xxiii] *Daily Mining Journal*, November 24, 1913.

[xxiv] *Marquette Chronicle*, June 4, 1819; *Evening News* (Sault Ste.Marie, Michigan), June 5, 1913.

[xxv] Welcome to the *USS Defender* - http://www.defender.navy.mil/default.aspx.

Went Missing Redux

C'est Le Guerre - The Inkermann *and* Cerisoles

[i] "It is the War"

[ii] This is speculation as the company records provide little insight to the arrangement.

[iii] Jeff Somner, H.B.A. "Launching Minesweepers at Can Car. 1918." Thunder Bay Historical Society, Papers and Records, Volume XVI (1988), pp. 32-40.

[iv] The LBP or Length Between Perpendiculars was 135.6 feet.

[v] Some sources claim five watertight compartments.

[vi] Vessel Dimension and Statistic Sheets, Fr. Peter Van der Linden, Marine Historical Society of Detroit.

[vii] From Pavia to Rocroi, The Tericios at War, http://www.geocities.com/ao1617/Battle.html; France Monthly, http://www.francemonthly.com/n/0503/index.php; The Battle of Inkermann, http://en.wikipedia.org/wiki/Battle_of_Inkerman; The Battle of Sebastapol, http://www.war-art.com/new_page_8.htm - The Battle of Cerisoles (1544) was a French victory against the Imperial army of Italy.

[vii] There is a legend that following the battle one of the captured Italian cannon ended up in the village of St. Paul. The people outside of the village (let's call them suburbanites) were jealous of the cannon and planned to assault the village and steal it. Hearing of the planned attack, the villagers (let's call them city slickers) prepared to defend their cannon but discovered while they had gunpowder, they didn't have any cannon balls. What can they do? Since the area was famous for cherries the governor sent the city folk out to find as many cherry pits as they could. Since the pits were still in the cherries, this meant doing a lot of munching and pit spitting. Eventually they had a huge pile of pits which, were duly loaded into the cannon and when the suburbanites finally launched their assault they were greeted by a hail of cherry pits! The first wave of attackers broke and ran, yelling "it's the pits, run for it!" Confused by the relentless "pitting," they all fled into the hills. Today the famous cannon is part of the old village wall, it's role in military history finished forever. It is thought by some researchers this is where the expression, "Ah, pit off" comes from although it also could have corrupted by a lisping French officer during the Franco-Prussian War (1870-71) to it's more common form today. But I digress.

End Notes

The Battle of Inkermann, was fought during the Crimean War, on November 5, 1854 and resulted in a British and French victory over Russian forces. During the battle British soldiers fought bravely and the fight was eventually won by a counter-attack by the French.

The Crimean War siege of Sebastapol (Sevastopol) was conducted 1854 - 1855. After the British Victory at The Battle of Alma, the British and French force advanced onto Sebastapol laying the Russian fortress under siege. After several Russian attempts to break out were beat back by the British the allies attempted to take the fortress by storm. The effort failed but constant British naval bombardment and dwindling Russian supplies gradually weakened the Czar's army. On September 8th the French seized a fortification at the south end of Sebastapol and three days later the Russians abandoned the fortress effectively ending the war.

[viii] Canadian Car and Foundry, http://ao.minisisinc.com/scripts/mwimain.dll/186/AUTH_WEB_NOSRCH/HEADING/Canadian+Car+and+Foundry?JUMP

[ix] Miamar Ship Index, http://www.miramarshipindex.org.nz/ship/show/59453.

[x] The actual number of crew on the *Inkermann* and *Sebastapol* could have been slightly different. There is some evidence the gunners mate from the *Sebastapol* was sent to the *Inkermann* to make room for the *Sebastapol's* second pilot, Lieutenant Leclerc to Captain Naval Attaché, c/o French Embassy, Washington.

[xi] *News-Chronicle* (Port Arthur, Ontario), November 15, 1918; *Daily Times* (Fort William, Ontario), December 6, 1918.

[xii] *Daily Times* (Fort William, Ontario) December 4, 1918.

[xiii] Investigation Into the Disappearance of the Minesweepers *Inkermann* and *Cerisoles*, Report by Lieutenant De. Chevigne, Assistant Naval Attache on His Mission to Canada, undated, pp. 66-67, Frederick Stonehouse Collection; it is assumed the "Helix" log is brand name for a patent log.

[xiv] Telegram, Consul General of France, December 4, 1919, Stonehouse Collection.

[xv] *News Chronicle* (Port Arthur, Ontario) December 10, 1918.

[xvi] *News Chronicle* (Port Arthur, Ontario) December 5, 1918.

WENT MISSING REDUX

[xvii]*News Chronicle* (Port Arthur, Ontario), December 11, 1918

[xviii]Log, Coast Guard Station Grand Marais, Michigan December 3, 1918, NARA; Report, Lt. Leclerc, Loss of *Inkermann* and *Cerisoles*, p. 15-16, Stonehouse Collection.

[xix]Report, Lt. Leclerc, Loss of the INKEMANN and *Cerisoles*, p. 17, Stonehouse Collection.

[xx]There is some confusion whether he left the *Sebastapol* at Kingston or Montreal. Regardless, Ensign Aubrey, a French officer who took an earlier minesweeper through, was directed to assume command of *Sebastapol* so Leclerc could take charge of the immediate search - Telegram to Lt. Leclerc, November 29, 1918; Telegram from Navy, Paris December 2, 1918, Stonehouse Collection; Investigation Into the Disappearance of the Minesweepers *Inkermann* and *Cerisoles*, Report by Lieutenant De. Chevigne, Assistant Naval Attache on His Mission to Canada, undated, pp. 11-14, Frederick Stonehouse Collection.

[xxi]Some sources use the name Garreau.

[xxii]*News Chronicle* (Port Arthur, Ontario), December 6, 1918.

[xxiii]Report, Lt. Leclerc, Loss of the INKEMANN and *Cerisoles*, p. 17, Stonehouse Collection.

[xxiv]Daily Log, U.S. Coast Guard Station Grand Marais, Michigan November 1918, NARA: Various newspaper accounts included a new lifeboat in the collection of items found by the Coast Guard on the beach. However, no mention of the lifeboat was made in the official log.

[xxv]Daily Log of Two-Heart River Coast Guard Station, December 3-10, 1918; What happened to the yawl is an open question. Was it returned to the French, or appropriated by a local fisherman or just left to rot behind the dunes?

[xxvi]Telegram, Navy, Paris, December 11, 1912, Stonehouse Collection.

[xxvii]Telegram, Navy, Paris, December 15, 1918, Stonehouse Collection.

[xxviii]*News Chronicle* (Port Arthur, Ontario), December 6, 1918; *Daily Times* (Fort William, Ontario), December 6, 1918.

[xxix]Hoyt, Edwin P. *The Last Explorer*. New York: John Day Company, 1968, 76-93.

End Notes

[xxx]John H. Bryant and Harold N. Cones. *Dangerous Crossings*. (Annapolis: Naval Institute Press, 2000), pp. 26,54,57,70-76, 142-143.

[xxxi]One of the Naval aviators under Byrd was Floyd Bennett. He piloted during his attempt to fly over the pole in 1926, a feat earning him the Medal of Honor. Bennett and Byrd were going to attempt to win the Orteig prize in 1927 to be awarded for the first nonstop flight from the U.S. to France. During a test flight the plane crashed, badly injuring Bennett. Lindbergh later succeeded in making the very difficult flight. Bennett later died from his injuries. By any standard he was a true American hero. Byrd later made a transatlantic flight a month after Lindbergh. Lt. Commander Donald B. MacMillan made 31 exploration trips to the Arctic and lived to the age of 95 passing in 1970. He made his last trip at age 80! Lt. Commander Eugene F. McDonald continued to live life to the fullest. In 1928 he led a trip to Lake Superior's Isle Royale resulting in eventual National Park designation. The *Inkermann, Cerisoles* and *Sebastapol* passed the north tip of the island on their run to the Soo. He was also involved in one of the many *Griffon* discoveries. Surely no Great Lakes shipwreck has been found more often in more places than the old *Griffon*! Lt. Commander Richard E. Byrd would lead a number of expeditions to the North and South Poles and is credited with being the first person to fly over the later. He died in 1957.

[xxxii]Vessel Dimensions and Statistic Sheet, Fr. Peter Van der Linden, Marine Historical Society of Detroit - *Bautzen*; Woolford, Arthur M. *Charting the Inland Seas: A History of the U.S. Lake Survey*. Detroit: U.S. Army Corps of Engineers, 1991, pp. 107-108,133.

[xxxiii]Vessel Dimensions and Statistic Sheet, Fr. Peter Van der Linden, Marine Historical Society of Detroit.

[xxxiv]Royal, Dominion and Indian Navy Ships, http://www.naval-history.net/xDKWW2-4107-34RNOverseas-Dominion.htm, her commander at the time was Lt A H Gott Royal Australian Navy Volunteer Reserve; Lenton, H.T. and Colledge, J.J., *British and Dominion Warships of World War II*. New York: Doubleday and Company, 1964, p. 322-323.

[xxxv]As we know little of Leclerc's experience or professional qualifications this is speculation. He may have been a grizzled master mariner pressed into French service or in contrast a green yachtsman pushed to the limit of his ability by the lack of real officers. However his conflict with his pilots regarding formation sailing would lead me to believe he was very much a

naval officer though perhaps with a higher opinion of himself than his actual experience and ability warranted.

[xxxvi] Sailors Bones - http://www.wildheart-ventures.com/mich_home.html#Bones; The tale does bear an uncanny similarity to the discovery of fake *Edmund Fitzgerald* life ring on Keweenaw Point in August 2007.

[xxxvii] Richard Ticknor. "The Sinking of the French Minesweepers *Inkermann* and *Cerisoles* in 1918." *Thunder Bay Historical Museum Society Papers and Records*, Volume 1, 1973, p. 4.

Addendum To Inkermann *and* Cerisoles

[i] Naval Mines - http://en.wikipedia.org/wiki/Naval_mine; Mine Neutralization - http://www.fas.org/man/dod-101/sys/ship/weaps/mine_sweep.htm; German Mines - http://images.google.com/imgres?imgurl=http://www.navweaps.com/Weapons/WAMGER_Mines_Emine_pic.jpg&imgrefurl=http://www.navweaps.com/Weapons/WAMGER_Mines.htm&h=381&w=417&sz=22&hl=en&start=3&um=1&tbnid=X9N0Ij2UPM0rqM:&tbnh=114&tbnw=125&prev=/images%3Fq%3Dhorned%2Bmines%26svnum%3D10%26um%3D1%26hl%3Den%26sa%3DG.

[ii] *Relevance, the Quarterly Journal of the Great War Society* - http://www.worldwar1.com/tgws/usnwwone.htm;

[iii] Mine Sweeping Tale of High Seas Surfaces With Trunk - http://www.lkwdpl.org/lore/lore126.htm.

[iv] *Relevance, the Quarterly Journal of the Great War Society* - http://www.worldwar1.com/tgws/usnwwone.htm.

[v] World War I Standard Built Ships - http://www.mariners-l.co.uk/WWIShipBuildersUSA.htm.

[vi] Canadian Navy Heritage Site - http://www.navy.forces.gc.ca/project_pride/photo_archive/photo_archive_description_page_e.asp?ImgNegNum=PA-192357; Great Lakes Foundry Almost Forgotten Aviation Magazine - http://www.vanguardcanada.com/CANCARThomas; PORT ARTHUR SHIPBUILDING FONDS RECORDS GROUP 5 - http://www.marmuseum.ca/findingaids/PASCOL2.html#WORLD%20WAR

End Notes

%20I; Ken Macpherson and John Burgess, *The Ships of Canada's Naval Forces 1910-1985*, Toronto; Collins, pp. 20-21, 144, 205-206.;

[vii] Report of Lieutenant De Chevigne to Commander De Saint Seine, Stonehouse Collection.

[viii] Who else accompanied the Lieutenant is unknown.

[ix] We don't know whether Parks was present in Fort William or had direct knowledge of the situation. He may have simply been relating what he heard.

[x] Investigation Into the Disappearance of the Minesweepers *Inkermann* and *Cerisoles*, Report by Lieutenant De. Chevigne, Assistant Naval Attaché on His Mission to Canada, undated, Frederick Stonehouse Collection.

[xi] The translation of the report uses the term "false maneuver." Considering the situation I can only reason this to be a "broach," which is swinging into the wind through bad steering or by the force of a heavy sea. It is a very dangerous situation and frequently the cause of foundering.

[xii] Trawlers commonly set a small jib sail to help steady the craft certain conditions.

[xiii] I can imagine the "words" the pilots had with Leclerc. They survive a broaching, broken steering, flooded engine and boiler rooms, loose deck cargo, likely a seasick crew and a know it all "captain" in very small vessel.

[xiv] Metacentric height is the distance from the center of gravity to the metacenter. The metacenter is the point of intersection between a vertical line passing through the center of a vessel upright and a vertical line passing through the center of gravity of the displaced water of a vessel, listed or heeled. If the metacenter is above the center of gravity, the vessel has stability; if separated by an insufficient distance, she is crank, and if below she is unstable. The point is the minesweepers were not overly stable but neither were they dangerous according to the architects at least.

[xv] This wasn't such a strange idea. When the British battleship *HMS Prince of Wales* left the shipyard in 1940 to fight the German battleship *Bismark* she carried a contingent of civilian workers to finish up required work. While the *Prince of Wales* survived her encounter with the *Bismark* she was raked pretty good, placing the civilians in harms's way.

[xvi] "Fish Holds" were center compartments on the ship accessible from the deck. Since the trawler design was very close to that of a civilian fishing vessel the term was commonly applied.

[xvii] Much of Leclerc's criticism can be explained by the requirements of Great Lakes sailing versus the open ocean. Common practice in one doesn't equal success in the other. It is worth noting that the egotistical Leclerc did manage to lose two ships while not listening to his pilots.

[xviii] The Spanish Flu of 1918 - http://www.mysteriesofcanada.com/Canada/spanish_flu_of_1918.htm, The Spanish Flu was first discovered in Spain in May 1918, thus the name. By September it was in North America, which would ultimately suffer approximately 25 million deaths. Worldwide the figure was placed at as many as 100 million. By contrast 9.3 million military men perished in World War I, 1914-18.

[xix] Lieutenant Leclerc to Captain Naval Attaché c/o French Embassy, Washington, Stonehouse Collection.

[xx] Lieutenant Leclerc to Captain Naval Attaché c/o French Embassy, Washington, Stonehouse Collection.

[xxi] Report of Lieutenant De Chevigne to Commander De Saint Seine, Stonehouse Collection.

Too Small To Do The Job - The Lambton

[i] This is of course a joke... but it does epitomize the purpose of a lighthouse.

[ii] St. Ignace Light on Talbot Island in western Lake Superior was known as the "Lighthouse of Doom" since three lightkeepers were killed either trying to leave in fall or in attempting to winter over. Located in the extreme northwest of the lake, it is an extremely isolated light. The Canadians finally abandoned it, perhaps in part due to the difficulty of finding keepers for a place with such an unsavory reputation.; Frederick Stonehouse. *Haunted Lakes II, More Great Lakes Ghost Stories*. (Duluth: Lake Superior Port Cities, 2000), pp. 23-26.

[iii] Thomas E. Appleton. *Usque Ad Mare, A History of the Canadian Coast Guard and Marine Services*, (Ottawa: Department of Transportation, 1968), pp. 251-254.

End Notes

[iv]Log of the U.S. Coast Guard Cutter *Cook*, April - May 1909.

[v]There is some confusion as the steamer *Franz* also reported being in the ice with the *Lambton*.

[vi]Ice can damage an unprotected rudder by working under and around it with the result of forcing the rudder out of its mounting. Ice can also damage propellers.

[vii]*Toronto Globe*, April 25, 1922.

[viii]*Saulte Star* (Saulte Ste. Marie, Ontario), December 18, 1916.

BIBLIOGRAPHIC NOTES

Captain Napier's Last Trip - The Alpena

Bowen, Dana Thomas, *Shipwrecks of the Lakes*, Cleveland: Freshwater Press, 1971.

Boyer, Dwight Dana, *Great Stories of the Great Lakes*, New York: Dodd, Mead and Company, 1966.

Chicago Daily News, October-December 1880.

Chicago Tribune, October-December 1880.

Daily Evening Herald (St. Joseph and Benton Harbor), July 19, 1881.

Elliot, James L. *Red Stacks Over the Horizon*. Grand Rapids: William B. Eerdmanns Publishing Company, 1967.

Heyl, Erik. *Early American Steamers*. Buffalo: Erik Heyl, 1969.

Holland City News, October-November 1880.

Lakeshore Commerce (Saugatuck, Michigan), October-November 1880.

Loss of the *Sultana* - http://www.navyandmarine.org/ondeck/1862sultana.htm.

Mansfield, John B. (ed. and compiler). *History of the Great Lakes*. Chicago: J.H. Beers and Company, 1899.

Pitz, Herbert. *Lake Michigan Disasters*. Manitowoc, Wisconsin, 1925.

Runge Collection, Wisconsin Marine History.

Sherman, Elizabeth. *Beyond the Windswept Dunes, the Story of Maritime Muskegon*, Detroit: Wayne State University Press, 2003.

Shipwrecks - http://boatnerd.com.

Went Missing Redux

Lost Off The Keweenaw, the Manistee

Ashland Press, November 24, December 1, 8, 15, 22, 1883; January 5, May 17, August 16, 1884; May 30, June 6, 13, 28, 1885.

Boyer, Dwight. *Great Stories of the Great Lakes*. New York: Dodd, Mead and Company, 1966.

Buffalo Express, May 29, 1885.

Correspondence with the National Archives and Records Service, dated March 4, 1976.

Portage Lake Mining Gazette (Houghton, Michigan), November 22, 29, December 6, 1883.

Ivan Walton Collection, Bentley Historical Library, University of Michigan, Box 6.

Iron Agitator (Ishpeming, Michigan), December 8, 1883.

Journal of the Light Station at Eagle Harbor, November 1883.

Lytle, William M. *Merchant Steam Vessels of the United States*. New York: Steamship Historical Society of America, 1952.

Mansfield, John B. (editor and compiler). *History of the Great Lakes*. Chicago: J.H. Beers and Company, 1899.

Mining Journal (Marquette, Michigan). November 17, 24, December 1, 22, 1883; June 9, 1884.

Mason, George C. "A Partial List of Hull Numbers of Ships Built by the Component Shipyards Making Up the American Shipbuilding Company, Cleveland, Ohio." *Inland Seas*, Winter 1952.

Mining Journal Vessel Register, 1877 - 1883.

Mitchell, C. Bradford, editor, *Merchant Steam Vessels of the United States, 1790 - 1863, the Lytle-Holdcamper List*. Staten Island, New York: The Steamship Historical Society of America, 1975.

Negaunee Iron Herald (Negaunee, Michigan), July 3, 1883.

Runge Collection. Wisconsin Marine Historical Society, Milwaukee Public Library, Milwaukee, Wisconsin.

Saginaw News (Saginaw, Michigan). November 23, 24, 1883.

Bibliographic Notes

Superior Times (Superior, Wisconsin). November 24, December 29, 1883.

Wolff, Julius F. "Some Noted Shipwrecks of the Michigan Coast of Lake Superior." *Inland Seas*, Fall, 1960.

Questions, Always Questions - The W.H. Gilcher

Annual Report, Lake Carriers Association, 1910.

Bowen, Dana Thomas. *Shipwrecks of the Lakes*. Cleveland: Freshwater Press, 1971.

Boyer, Dwight. *Great Stories of the Great Lakes*. New York: Dodd, Mead and Company, 1966.

Carus, Captain Edward. *100 Years of Disasters on the Great Lakes*. Unpublished Manuscript, 1931.

Chicago Inter-Ocean, November 2, 5, 1892.

Cleveland Press, November 2 - 5, 1893.

Daily Log, U.S. Life-Saving Station at North Manitou Island, October 28-31, 1892.

Detroit Free Press, November 5, 11, 1892.

Duluth News Tribune, November 25, 1892.

Leelanau Enterprise, January 5, 1893, June 12, 2007.

Manistee Times-Sentinel, November 11, 1892.

Mansfield, John B. (ed. and compiler). *History of the Great Lakes*. Chicago: J.H. Beers and Company, 1899.

Marine Review, February 18, September 12, December 25, 1892.

Muskegon Daily Chronicle, November 1892.

Naval Architectural Drawings, American Shipbuilding Company and Predecessors, 1867-1920, MS-212, Center for Archival Collections, Bowling Green State University, July 1983.

Pitz, Herbert. *Lake Michigan Disasters*. Manitowoc, 1925.

Runge Collection, Marine Historical Society of Wisconsin.

Time Magazine, August 19, 1929.

Went Missing Redux

Vrana, Kenneth J. *Inventory of Maritime and Recreational Resources of the Manitou Passage Underwater Preserve.* Lansing: Department of Park, Recreation and Tourism Resources, 1995, pp. 4-81-4-82.

Wright, Richard J. *Freshwater Whales, A History of the American Shipbuilding Company and its Predecessors.* Kent State University Press, 1969.

Wisconsin Shipwrecks - http://www.wisconsinshipwrecks.org/explore_oconnor_final2.cfm

Marine History of the Great Lakes - http://www.hhpl.on.ca/GreatLakes/Wrecks/details.asp?ID=22456

Addendum To Cracking - Gilcher

Embrittlement is a loss of elasticity of a material, making it brittle.

Ductility is the mechanical property of being capable of sustaining large plastic deformations due to tensile stress without fracture. For example metal being drawn into wire.

Liberty Ship - http://en.wikipedia.org/wiki/Liberty_ship" Prediction of ship brittle fracture casualty rates by a probabilistic method - http://www.sciencedirect.com/science?_ob=ArticleURL&_udi=B6V41-4FY9M86-2&_user=10&_coverDate=12%2F31%2F2004&_rdoc=1&_fmt=&_orig=search&_sort=d&view=c&_acct=C000050221&_version=1&_urlVersion=0&_userid=10&md5=d79053d576b28f20422db017028f95e7"

Structural Problems - http://www.probusmossvale.org.au/Military%20History_files/Liberty%20Ships/LIBERTY%20SHIPS2.htm.

Cold Water Sinks *Titanic* - http://www.disastercity.info/titanic/index.shtml.

Physics Forum - http://www.physicsforums.com/archive/index.php/t-105378.html.

Metallurgy of the RMS *Titanic* - http://www.metallurgy.nist.gov/webpages/TFoecke/titanic/Titanic.pdf.

FAQs Steel - http://titanic.marconigraph.com/faqs3.html.

Bibliographic Notes

Lost Off The Keweenaw, The Hudson

Annual Report of the U.S. Life-Saving Service, 1902.

Annual Report of the U.S. Steamboat Inspection Service, 1902.

Beacons in the Night, Clarke Historical Library - http://clarke.cmich.edu/lighthouses/lhkeep1.htm

Beeson, Harvey Childs, *Beeson's Inland Marine Directory*. Chicago: Harvey C. Beeson, 1902.

Buffalo Express, September - November 1901.

Buffalo Evening News, September - November 1901.

Buffalo Commercial, September - November 1901

Carus, Captain Edward. *100 Years of Disasters of the Great Lakes*. Unpublished Manuscript, 1931.

Daily Mining Gazette (Houghton, Michigan), September - November 1901.

Detroit Free Press, November 29, December 3,6,9, 1898: October 4,21, 26, November 12,17, 1899.

Duluth News-Tribune, September - December 1901.

Evening News (Saulte St. Marie, Michigan), November 5, 1904.

Log of the Light-Station at Eagle River, September 1901.

Mining Journal (Marquette, Michigan), September - October 1901.

Overfield, Joseph M. *The Last Voyage of the* Hudson. Kenmore, NY: Ken-Ton Printing Company, 1981.

Runge Collection, Milwaukee Public Library, Milwaukee, Wisconsin.

Scanner, Toronto Marine Historical Society, April 1980.

Stonehouse, Frederick. *Haunted Lakes, Great Lakes Ghost Stories, Superstitions and Sea Serpents*, Duluth: Lake Superior Port Cities, 1997.

Tag, Thomas and Phyllis. The Lighthouse Keepers of Lake Superior, Dayton, Ohio: Great Lakes Lighthouse Research, nd.

Tioga - Stonehouse Collection.

Wolff, Julius F. "They Sailed Away on Lake Superior." *Inland Seas*, Winter, 1973.

WENT MISSING REDUX

A Victim Of Superior Shoal? - **Bannockburn**

Annual Report of the U.S. Life-Saving Service, 1902.

Barry, James P. *Ships of the Great Lakes.* Berkley, California: Howell-North Books, 1970

Beeson, Harvey C. *Beeson's Inland Marine Directory*. Chicago: Harvey C. Beeson, 1970.

Canadian List of Shipping, 1901.

Carus, Captain Edward, *100 Years of Disasters on the Great Lakes*. Unpublished Manuscript, 1931.

Canadian Transportation Ministry Archives.

Correspondence with the National Maritime Museum, Greenwich, U.K. dated October 1976.

Curwood, James Oliver. "The Perils of Navigation on the Great Lakes," *Inland Seas*, Winter 1970.

Daily Mining Journal (Marquette, Michigan). November 27 - 29, December 1, 2, 1902.

Duluth News-Tribune, November 27-30, December 1, 13, 1902.

Fillmore, Stanley and Sandilands, R.W. *The Chartmakers, the History of Nautical Surveying in Canada*. NC Press Limited, 1983.

Friends of the Canadian Hydrograpy, http://www.canfoh.org/Ships/Bayfield.htm#II.

Journal of the Life-Saving Station at Grand Marais, Michigan, December 12-20, 1902.

Landon, Fred. "The Loss of the *Bannockburn*." *Inland Seas*, Winter 1957.

Mining Gazette (Houghton, Michigan), November 28 - 29, 1902.

Stonehouse, Frederick. *Went Missing*. Gwinn, Michigan: Avery Color Studios, 1984.

U.S. Lake Survey, *Survey of the Northern and Northwestern Lakes, Great Lakes Pilot*, 1955.

Wolff, Julius F. "They Sailed Away on Lake Superior," *Inland Seas*, Winter 1973.

Bibliographic Notes

"Freshwater, Bah!" - *The* Adella Shores

Annual Report of the U.S. Life-Saving Service, 1910.

Aurania File, Stonehouse Collection.

Aurania - http://www.boatnerd.com.

Annual Report, U.S. Life-Saving Service, 1910.

Daily Log, U.S. Life-Saving Station - Grand Marais, Michigan, May 1909.

Daily Mining Journal (Marquette, Michigan), May 8 - 11, 1909.

Duluth Evening Herald, May 8, 9, 11, 21, 1909.

Duluth News Tribune, December 2, 1901; May 8, 9, 11, 21, 1909.

Evening News (Sault Ste. Marie, Michigan) May 8, 9, 12, 1909.

Free Press (Detroit), December 17, 1909.

Nor'Easter, Journal of the Lake Superior Marine Museum Association, Volume 21, Number 1, January - February 1996.

Runge Collection, Wisconsin Marine Historical Society.

Stonehouse, Frederick. *Lighthouse Keepers and Coast Guard Cutters*. Gwinn, Michigan: Avery Color Studios; Gwinn, Michigan, 2000.

Telescope. January-February 1993, p. 3.

Wolff, Julius F. "They Sailed Away on Lake Superior," *Inland Seas*, Winter 1973.

"Bucking Into The Teeth Of The Gale - The Henry B. Smith

American Shipbuilding Company, "Profile and Deck Plans of Hull 342-343," September 25, 1905.

American Shipbuilding Company, "Cabin and Hull Plan 343-343," November 3, 1905.

Annual Report of the U.S. Life-Saving Service, 1913, 1914.

Annual Report of the U.S. Steamboat Inspection Service, 1914.

Barcus, Frank, *Freshwater Fury*, Detroit: Wayne State University Press, 1960.

Beeson, Harvey C. *Beeson's Inland Marine Directory 1913.*

Brown, David G. *White Hurricane.* Chicago: International Marine, 2002.

Daily Mining Gazette (Houghton, Michigan), November 13-16, 19, 23, 1913.

Daily Mining Journal (Marquette, Michigan), November 9-11, 15-20, 22-25, 1913. June 4, 1914.

E-mail, Paul W. Schopp to author, June 8, 1997.

Evening News (Sault Ste. Marie, Michigan), November 9, 13, 14, 22, 23, December 3, 1913.

Greenwood. John O. *The Fleet Histories, Volume Six*, Cleveland: Freshwater Press, 1998.

"Journal of the Life-Saving Station at Grand Marais," NARA, November 10-13, 1913.

"Journal of the Life-Saving Station at Marquette," NARA, November 9-11, 1913

"Journal of the Life-Saving Station at Vermilion," NARA, November, 1913

Ludington Daily News, November 3, 1983.

Marquette Chronicle (Marquette, Michigan), June 4, 1914.

Merchant Vessels of the U.S. various issues.

Milwaukee Journal, November 1913.

Steamship *J.B. Ford* - http://www.steamshipjbfordhistoricalsurvey.com/.

U.S. Department of Agriculture and Weather Bureau, Daily Local Record, Marquette, Michigan, November 6 - 10, 1913.

Welcome to the USS Defender - http://www.defender.navy.mil/default.aspx.

"Wreck Report, U.S. Life-Saving Service, Steamer *Henry B. Smith*," NARA, November 26, 1913.

C'est Le Guerre - The Inkermann *and* Cerisoles

Annual Report of the Lake Carrier's Association, 1918.

Bryant, John H. and. Cones, Harold N. *Dangerous Crossings.* (Annapolis:

Bibliographic Notes

Naval Institute Press), 2000.

Canadian Car and Foundry, http://ao.minisisinc.com/scripts/mwimain.dll/186/AUTH_WEB_NOSRCH/HEADING/Canadian+Car+and+Foundry?JUMP.

Certificate of Enrollment, Steamer *Rowena*, 1923.

Correspondence, Mr. L. W. Moore of the Port of Lowestaft Research Society, Diss. England, with author, dated April 3, 1976.

Correspondence, Wheelhouse Maritime Museum, Ottawa, with author, dated January 19, 1975.

Daily Mining Gazette (Houghton, Michigan), December 5, 13, 27, 1918.

Daily Mining Journal (Marquette, Michigan), December 5, 6, 1918.

Daily Times-Journal (Fort William, Ontario), December 4, 1957.

Evening News (Saulte St. Marie, Michigan) December 4-16, 1918.

France Monthly, http://www.francemonthly.com/n/0503/index.php.

From Pavia to Rocroi, The Tericios at War - http://www.geocities.com/ao1617/Battle.html.

French Naval Archives, Paris, France.

Hoyt, Edwin P. *The Last Explorer*. New York: John Day Company, 1968, 76-93.

Jane's Fighting Ships of World War I. New York: Military Press, 1990, 200-201.

Lake Superior Marine Museum Archive, Duluth, Minnesota.

Lenton, H.T. and Colledge, J.J., *British and Dominion Warships of World War II*. New York: Doubleday and Company, 1964, p. 322-323.

Letter to the Editor, Ronald F. Beaupre, *Inland Seas*, Winter 1986, p. 294.

Log of Coast Guard Station Number 296 (Grand Marais, Michigan), December 3-9, 1918.

Macpherson, Ken and Burgess, John, *The Ships of Canada's Naval Forces 1910-1985*. Toronto: Collins, 1981, pp. 20-22, 144, 205-206.

Miamar Ship Index http://www.miramarshipindex.org.nz/ship/show/59453.

News Chronicle (Port Arthur, Ontario), December 3-16, 1918.

Report, Lt. Leclerc, Loss of *Inkermann* and *Cerisoles*, p. 15-17, Stonehouse Collection.

Report, Lt. Leclerc to Captain Naval Attache, c/o French Embassy, Washington, Stonehouse Collection.

Royal, Dominion and Indian Navy Ships - http://www.naval-history.net/xDKWW2-4107-34RNOverseas-Dominion.htm.

Sailors Bones - http://www.wildheart-ventures.com/mich_home.html#Bones.

Somner, Jeff, H.B.A. "Launching Minesweepers at Can Car. 1918." *Thunder Bay Historical Society, Papers and Records*, Volume XVI (1988), pp. 32-40.

Telegram, Consul General of France, December 4, 1919, Stonehouse Collection.

Telegram, Navy, Paris December 2, 1918.

Telegram, Navy, Paris, December 15, 1918, Stonehouse Collection.

Telegram, Navy, Paris, December 11, 1912, Stonehouse Collection.

Telegram, Lt. Leclerc, November 29, 1918, Stonehouse Collection.

Ticknor, Richard J. "The Sinking of the French Minesweepers *Inkermann* and *Cerisoles* in 1918," Thunder Bay Historical Museum Society Papers and Records, Volume 1," 1973, 1-4.

The Battle of Inkermann - http://en.wikipedia.org/wiki/Battle_of_Inkerman.

The Battle of Sebastapol - http://www.war-art.com/new_page_8.htm.

Times Journal (Fort William, Ontario), December 3-11, 1918.

Wolff, Julius F. "The Sailed Away on Lake Superior." *Inland Seas*, Winter 1973.

Wrigley, Ronald. *Shipwrecked, Vessels That Met Tragedy on Northern Lake Superior*. Cobalt, Ontario: Highway Book Shop.

Too Small To Do The Job - The Lambton

Appleton, Thomas E. *Usque Ad Mare, A History of the Canadian Coast*

Bibliographic Notes

Guard and Marine Services. Ottawa: Department of Transportation, 1968.

Canadian Public Archives, Ottawa.

Daily Mining Journal (Marquette, Michigan), April 20, 25, 26, 1922.

Holland, Francis Ross. *America's Lighthouses.* Battlesboro, Vermont: Stephen Green Press, 1972.

Log of the U.S. Coast Guard Cutter *Cook*, April - May 1909.

Maginley, Charles D. and Collin, Bernard, *The Ships of Canada's Marine Services.* St. Chatherines, Ontario: Vanwell Publishing Limited, 2001, pp. 54, 65.

O'Brien, T. Michael, *Guardians of the Eighth Sea, A History of the U.S. Coast Guard on the Great Lakes.* n.d.

Report of J. N. Arthurs Concerning the Loss of the *C.G.S. Lambton*, dated May 2, 1922; *Lambton* - Stonehouse Collection.

Saulte Star (Saulte Ste. Marie, Ontario), December 18, 1916

Stonehouse, Frederick *Haunted Lakes II, More Great Lakes Ghost Stories*, Duluth: Lake Superior Port Cities, 2000.

Toronto Globe, April 20, 25, 26, 1922.

Van der Linden, Rev. Peter, ed. *Great Lakes Ships We Remember II*, Cleveland: Freshwater Press, 1979.

ABOUT THE AUTHOR

Frederick Stonehouse holds a Master of Arts Degree in History from Northern Michigan University, Marquette, Michigan, and has authored many books on Great Lakes maritime history. He is the 2006 recipient of the Association for Great Lakes Maritime History Award for Historic Interpretation and received the 2007 Marine Historical Society of Detroit Historian of the Year Award. *Steel On The Bottom, Great Lakes Shipwrecks, Great Lakes Crime,*  *Murder, Mayhem, Booze & Broads, Lake Superior's "Shipwreck Coast," Dangerous Coast: Pictured Rocks Shipwrecks, The Wreck Of The Edmund Fitzgerald, Great Lakes Lighthouse Tales, Women And The Lakes, Untold Great Lakes Maritime Tales, Women And The Lakes II, More Untold Great Lakes Maritime Tales, Final Passage, True Shipwreck Adventures, My Summer At The Lighthouse, A Boy's Journal* and *Cooking Lighthouse Style, Favorite Recipes From Coast To Coast* are all published by Avery Color Studios, Inc.

He has also been a consultant for both the U.S. National Park Service and Parks Canada, and an "on air" expert for National Geographic Explorer and the History Channel as well as many regional media productions. He has taught Great Lakes Maritime History at Northern Michigan University and is an active consultant for numerous Great Lakes oriented projects and programs. Check www.frederickstonehouse.com for more details.

His articles have been published in numerous publications including *Skin Diver, Great Lakes Cruiser Magazine* and *Lake Superior Magazine*. He is a member of the Board of Directors of the Marquette Maritime Museum and a member of the Board of Directors of the United States Life Saving Service Heritage Association.

Stonehouse resides in Marquette, Michigan.

Other Fred Stonehouse titles by Avery Color Studios, Inc.

- *Steel On The Bottom, Great Lakes Shipwrecks*
- *Great Lakes Crime, Murder, Mayhem, Booze & Broads*
- *Great Lakes Crime II, More Murder, Mayhem, Booze & Broads*
- *The Wreck Of The Edmund Fitzgerald*
- *Women And The Lakes, Untold Great Lakes Maritime Tales*
- *Women And The Lakes II, More Untold Great Lakes Maritime Tales*
- *Great Lakes Lighthouse Tales*
- *Lake Superior's Shipwreck Coast*
- *Dangerous Coast: Pictured Rock Shipwrecks*
- *Cooking Lighthouse Style, Favorite Recipes From Coast To Coast*
- *My Summer At The Lighthouse, A Boy's Journal*
- *Final Passage, True Shipwreck Adventures*

Avery Color Studios, Inc. has a full line of Great Lakes oriented books, puzzles, cookbooks, shipwreck and lighthouse maps, lighthouse posters and Fresnel lens model.

For a full color catalog call:
1-800-722-9925

Avery Color Studios, Inc. products are available at gift shops and bookstores throughout the Great Lakes region.